I0476717

How to Start Your Own Business!

All You Need to Know to Easily Start Your Own Business for Less than $50!

By

Kimberly Peters

For

The Customer Service

Training Institute

Contents

Introduction

When it comes to dreams about our future financial prosperity, the thought of owning our own business pops into the heads of a lot of people. The thought of earning a huge income and creating something that will help pave the way for a secure and expensive lifestyle holds a lot of hope and promise for many people.

The fact that starting and creating your own business can become a reality for just about anyone, you have to go into the process with your eyes open and with the ability to answer some tough questions honestly and openly. If you can do that, you will save yourself a lot of time and trouble later on.

There are many ways you can start your own business. You can take an idea and turn it into a product or service and start selling it to other people. Behind every huge company there were people who had a simple idea or a great product that made that business possible. There is no reason why you cannot be the next success story.

Throughout this book you will find a lot of information and a healthy dose of reality because if you are going to have a legitimate shot at success, you must ALWAYS deal with reality. Hopes and dreams are not enough to be successful. You need a great idea or product and sometimes a bit of luck thrown in as well.

Though not all the material in this book might not apply to you and your situation, you should read every word anyway. Because you are bound to learn something or even just become aware of something that will help you down the road a bit. It is much easier, and also much cheaper, to learn from other people's mistakes instead of making those same mistakes yourself. So read every word and try and apply it in your life, your dreams and your own individual situation. You will save yourself a lot of wasted time and money if you will just do that.

The key to your success in creating your own business, as well as most everything else in life, is to try your best and always be honest with yourself along the way. There are good ideas that make their owners millions and there are some great ideas that don't sell at all. You need to know when you have a winner and to move ahead and also when you have a loser and learn to quit and start over.

That is the greatest obstacle that lies between you and your future success.

Everyone experiences failure at some points in their life so it is not a matter of avoiding failure because that is impossible. Instead, whether you are going to be a success or not often will depend on how you react to that failure and what you do next.

Successful people learn from their failures so they don't make the same mistake next time. Because of their failure they will do things differently moving forward and eliminate that cause of failure from happening again. You might say that this is a trial by error process and you would be exactly correct. You try, you fail, you make adjustments and you try again. That is how people become successful.

But if you stop trying, or even become so afraid of failure that you never try in the first place, you will never truly become successful or do your best in life. You need to put yourself "out there" and go after what you want in life. Most other people do that and if you don't, you will be left standing by the wayside.

You may find out that running your own business isn't for you and if that is the case that's just fine. Not everyone is cut out to own their own business just like some people are not cut out to be athletes or concert pianists.

But if that is something you dream about, then you owe it to yourself to at least investigate it further. That is why this book is going to become so valuable to you. We are going to show you what it takes, what lies ahead and what type of skills you are going to have I order to become a successful business owner. Then you can see if that is something you are still interested in.

But the truly wonderful thing about owning your own business is that you get to design the business to best suit YOUR needs. You can make it as large or as small as you want it and you can be totally involved and do everything or remove yourself from the picture by automating everything. The choice is yours and yours alone.

Another piece of great news is that it has never been easier to open your own business. Software tools are more in-depth yet easier to use than ever before and things that used to be reserved for the "major players" can now be within the reach of the small business owner working part time out of his or her parent's garage.

So as we move forward, remember that you can do this if you really want to. So keep an open mind and always make the decisions based on what YOU want and not by whatever someone else might say. This is going to be YOUR business so it should be run YOUR way and reflect who YOU are and what YOUR values might be.

A few words before we get started about how this book was put together. We have been writing business training manuals and materials for over 25 years and we have created a certain format that enables more people to get more out of the training in less time with better results. It has taken us a long time to arrive at this format but once we did, we started seeing people getting amazing results in less time than they ever thought possible.

Since many people who buy instructional or personal improvement books like this one have an immediate or very important need, most of these readers will jump ahead to those sections of the book. While that is perfectly fine, sometimes they might miss material presented earlier and not be able to fully understand what we are covering in that chapter they started with.

To help eliminate that problem we have done our best to create each chapter as a stand-alone chapter that contains all the material and knowledge necessary to understand what that chapter is all about. This helps people understand better and retain the information for longer periods of time.

Because of this approach you might see certain material repeated once or twice and this is not by accident or error.

Instead, we do it so that people can understand no matter where they start the book or whatever order they decide to read it in. Another benefit of this approach is that often the most important material is repeated and the more often you read something, the longer you will retain that particular information. Feel free to take notes as you go through the book as well. This will also greatly improve your understanding and increase the time that you will retain that information even more.

Last, but certainly not least, you are going to read a lot of information and techniques that will help you start and run your new business. But the best way of learning and understanding this new information is by taking what you have read and then turn it into something that is relevant to your situation and dreams. When you are able to do that, the material will jump off the pages and become real for you. That is when you will really learn the material that will help you start and operate a successful business.

Why Start Your Own Business?

Some people wonder why other people seem so committed to starting their own business. They don't see the reasons or rewards behind it and instead concentrate on the risks and negatives. But despite this, there are many reasons why some people get the entrepreneurial spirit and go out and start their own business.

Some of the reasons are very valid while other reasons contain perceptions or generalizations that might or might not be accurate or even valid. Plus, to confuse things even more, even the most valid and spot on reasons might not apply to certain people.

Most of the time the allure about owning your own business is the chance to have freedom to do what you want when you want without having to ask a boss or an owner for a day off or whether or not you can leave early. They honestly believe that since you are the owner or the boss you can set your own schedule and work when you want, if you want and forever long you want.

Another powerful reasons is that most people feel that owning your own business is the only way to achieve financial freedom and wealth in a relatively short period of time. They like the idea that instead of taking a salary or small commission, they will instead take 100% of the profits generated by the business. After all, 100% is almost always better than a lower percentage when it comes to profits!

Then there are people who are driven to improve something or solve a problem or deliver something brand new to the world. Even though no one else might share their dream or work hard to make it possible, they realize that they can do this all by themselves through their own business. This is exactly how some of the largest and most successful companies got their start. They took an idea and some passion and brought it to life.

Still others like the idea of being in greater control of one's destiny. In this age or corporate downsizing and layoffs, the idea of owning your own company and playing an active role in your future just makes sense. But even this is an oversimplification of the reality of business ownership.

Then we have the most interesting group of business owners and those are the people who could not get a job in the current labor market and faced with bills, mortgages and other expenses they took the bull by the horns and didn't wait for someone to hire them, they hired themselves.

Sometimes the worst possible situations can turn out to truly have a silver lining.

I think if you were to look at the most successful entrepreneurs today you would see a mixture or blend of several of these feelings or reasons in their past that caused them to "go it alone" and start their own business. This is because there are always reasons for what people do in their lives. All we have to do is look hard enough and long enough and we will find it.

But there is one thing that bonds all successful entrepreneurs together and that is their entrepreneurial spirit. That spirit that tells them that they can be successful even when everyone else tells them to go in another direction. These are the people who don't listen to the critics and just go out and achieve their dreams.

Owning your own business will have its own unique set of challenges and rough spots. But if the idea is right and the person is right, the rewards can be amazing. Besides the financial rewards and the increased control over ones destiny, you cannot beat the feeling of accomplishment you get when you see the business you created grow and grow over time.

So if you have the desire and the spirit and if you are willing to make the sacrifices and put in the effort required to build a successful spirit, then the future could very well look extremely bright for you and your family.

Are You the Right Type of Person?

While I do not like to burst anyone's bubble so early on, you need to determine first and foremost whether you are the type of person that can create and operate their own business. This is important because some of us are just not cut out for business ownership and it is much better to find out now rather than later when the business starts to falter.

People who start and run their own business need to have a certain set of skills and personality traits. Without any of these particular skills or traits the entire business will be at risk. With that in mind here are a list of some of the most important skills and traits that the business owner needs to have in order to start and build their own successful business:

Self-Starter

When you own your own business, you will need to know what needs to be done and when it needs to be done and you will have to make sure that you take care of business.

There will be no one around to show you what to do or tell you when something needs to be done. It is going to be up to you and only you to see that everything is taken care of.

If you are the type of person who needs to be shown the way or given specific instructions in order to complete a task you should reconsider starting your own business. That is because you will have to make all the decisions on your own without outside help or guidance.

If you are not a self-starter and do not work well without supervision but still want to start your own business, I suggest you take on a partner who can perform those functions and act as a managing partner to help you stay on track. Many business operate just fine with this type of arrangement. One partner takes care of the planning and implementation while the other handles the creative or product side. The key is knowing who you are and what you are capable of.

Detail Oriented

Starting and operating a business requires the attention to a million little details. From expenses to product design and placement to marketing and a host of other things, there is much to do and a lot of details involved.

Owning a business requires attention to the little things that many people think are not important. Little things such as deadlines and paperwork are critical to the overall success of a business.

Understanding what needs to happen and exactly how it should happen can make all the difference in the world when it comes to a small business.

This is especially true throughout the start-up phase where everything is new and when there are so many things that could go wrong if not done properly. As time goes on and the bugs all get worked out these little details may go away but in the beginning, it is the little things that can bring a business to its knees and it can happen very quickly.

Goal Oriented

Creating a business is more than taking a product or an idea and selling it to the masses. There are objectives to meet and goals to achieve. Goals are what you want the business to achieve within a certain period of time. Goals are important because they are the driving forces behind the day to day actions within your business.

Do you want to create a $100,000 a year business or a $100,000,000 a year business? This is important because the structure and policies of the business will need to support your growth and goals. In other words, you need to understand where you want to go and how to get to that point in the most efficient manner possible.

Goals are extremely important to a new business because they give you a perspective on how well you and your business are doing. For example, if you feel you can create a $1,000,000 a year business but 6 months into the business you have only sold $1,500 worth of product, you might be in serious trouble. But if your goals were to be at the $1,500 point 6 months in and at $50,000 by the end of the first year you might be on the right track.

Goals help keep you focused and on the right track. They show you when things are going well and when corrective measure might have to take place. If you are someone that doesn't believe in goals or feel they have little value, then you and your business might be in for a lot of trouble down the road. Especially in the very beginning.

High Degree of Common Sense

Throughout my career in the business world I have seen many person with a huge amount of book knowledge and advanced degrees fail miserably in the workplace. Not because they were not smart or lacked the required knowledge but because they were unable to take what they had learned and implement it in the real world.

Starting and running your own business take a lot of practical knowledge and common sense. Knowledge is one thing but actually using that knowledge is something else entirely.

You need to be able to use what you have learned in a real world environment.

The "real world" is not a perfect place. Things do not go as planned more often than not. The people who can take their knowledge and use it in an imperfect environment are the ones who will experience the most success. These are the people who will do what they think will work and will be able to evaluate and make adjustments along the way in order to get the best possible results.

Think about business and common sense in another way. The essence of any business is the ability to convince other people that they need and should purchase your products or services above anyone else's. In order to achieve that goal you are going to have to take a lot of different factors into consideration. Some of those factors are never going to be learned through books or courses, either.

Successful business owners take book or theoretical knowledge and combine it with common sense and practical knowledge. The result is a well thought out and practical business plan that will be able to get the results that people need in any given situation. It is the person who can use common sense in conjunction with other knowledge to get the best results possible in the shortest period of time.

Focused and Committed

Here is one of the most important traits a business owner needs to have. They need to be focused and committed to seeing things through to completion. It is very easy to get distracted or to be pulled in so many directions at one time that you lose focus. A business owner MUST be able to stay focused even while things going on around them are in chaos.

A business owner must keep one eye on the end goal while the other eye takes are of what is going on at that particular point in time. IN other words, a good business owner will keep focused on the long term goals or objectives while taking care of the day to day business activities. They will make sure everything that needs to be done is done and that everything is moving in the right direction both for today and for the future as well.

Analytical Skills

Not everyone who has a great idea or product is able to take that idea and create a business around it. After all, there is much more to running a profitable business than creating a great product. One of the skills sets most usually overlooked is the ability to analyze data and performance of the business during and after the start-up phase.

There are factors such as customer acquisition costs and cost per unit and taxes and other performance related data that must be understood before the business can move on to the next level. This data does not analyze itself and you will need someone who can take the raw data and analyze it so it makes sense.

A business owner must be able to understand profit and loss as well as sales data and customer satisfaction data. At any given time the business owner must be able to know if they are turning a profit or running at a loss. They must be able to understand which parts of their business are profitable and running well as opposed to the parts that are draining the business of its resources.

This is one of those areas that not even having a partner who knows these things is enough. You need to understand it as well so you can protect your interests in the business and not risk people cheating you without your knowledge.

If you currently do not have these skills, do not worry at this point. But do make the effort to learn them through either taking some courses or by doing some reading. If you hire a partner by all means go through this data with them so you understand it as well.

Ask questions until you are fairly certain that you know what is going on with your business at any given time. This is your business and you need to protect your interests in it.

Practical Skills

Since you are starting your own business, it is likely that it will be all on you or just a few people, to take care of everything that must be taken care of when it comes to starting and growing the business. So not only will you need to know what has to be done, you will need to know HOW to do all of those things as well.

You will probably not have the money or resources to outsourcing everything nor will you be able to afford all the employees need either. So it will be up to you to handle all the little things that go along with running a small business.

That means you will have to have some practical knowledge of sales, marketing, advertising, accounting, local laws and business regulations as well as packaging, shipping and customer service. While this does not mean you have to be at expert level on any or all of these, it does mean that you have to have at least a working knowledge of all of this plus a lot more for some businesses.

Practical knowledge means knowing who to call or contact for various situations or needs and how to get access to the things you and your business needs whenever you need it. It means being able to design a serviceable advertisement or understanding how to set up and use a basic website. Though there are people who can do this faster and better than you might be able to, they will cost you money that you might not have, especially at the beginning

You will also have to set up payment systems whether your business is a brick and mortar store or an online business. After all, people will need a way to pay for the products and services they want to buy. There are fees associated with these services so you should become knowledgeable about what your business needs and where to get it at the best cost.

At this point there is one more thing that a good business owner need to have in order to build and maintain a successful business.

And that one thing is.....................

You Need to Be Honest with Yourself

We all have known people who had an exaggerated opinion of their knowledge and skills. They thought they knew everything and that they were 100% capable of excelling at anything and everything they wanted. The problem is that most of these people did not have the skills or abilities to back up those claims.

Even the smartest or most qualified individual will have both strong points and weak points. In other words they will be great at some things, good at others, and weak or poor at other things as well. Very rare is it that someone is great at all parts of their life or business.

So it is not as important that you are great at everything as it is to really understand and acknowledge what your strong points are and what your weak points might be. That way we can deal with our weak points and either strengthen them or find ways to work around our weaknesses. This might mean outsourcing some things or bringing in partners or employees. Whatever the answer might be, we need to understand our needs before we can make the right decisions.

The problem is that a LOT or people, and probably you to some extent, are uncomfortable when it comes to admitting their flaws or weaknesses. We tend to keep them to ourselves and even try to convince ourselves that we have no weak points at all. This is where the real danger comes into play. Because when we own our own business, there usually is not someone in place who can see things objectively or how they really are.

There is one process that I strongly urge everyone considering starting their own business put themselves through. It is not a difficult process and when you are finished you should have a pretty good idea if you have what it takes to run a successful business. You should also have a good understand of where you weak points are and how you can strengthen them.

The process is called a "Business Skills Audit" and you can easily do one in the privacy of your own home. The only thing you need to do is be as honest and forthcoming as you possibly can with yourself throughout the process. If you are weak when it comes to some things, that's OK as long as you admit that to yourself.

Keep in mind that the results of this "audit" can be kept totally confidential.

That means the answers can be known only to yourself unless you feel that it might be beneficial for someone else to get involved with the process. But you can do this all by yourself and keep the answers or results known only to yourself. So if you lie or skate over some questions you are only hurting yourself. Just be honest and the results will really help you.

Here are a few questions you might ask yourself during this audit:

Can I work well without supervision?

This means "Do you have what it takes to do what needs to be done without someone reminding you or telling you to do something. It is amazing how many people need someone to keep them on track and on task. If you do not work well without supervision then you should seriously consider getting a partner to help you. No one who lets things slide will likely ever be as successful as they could be in their own business.

Do I follow through on tasks to completion?

This refers to your ability to see things through until the very end and not stopping when things get difficult or when they appear to be "good enough".

Often the difference between success and failure is taking everything and doing your very best to create the best business, the best products and the best customer service. This cannot be attained by anyone who stops as soon as they think they can.

Am I good when it comes to making changes on the move when things don't go as planned?

Nothing in business goes according to plan. While a good plan will make things easier and help you grow your business fast and accurately, things are always going to happen. There is so much that is out of your direct control when it comes to business that you always have to be ready to spot the need for change and make those changes on the fly.

If you are a regimented or inflexible kind of person that will place your ability to deal with problems at risk. The longer you take to spot a problem and take corrective action the more it is going to cost you and your business. Taken to the extreme, if you are so inflexible and think that your plan is perfect and refuse to make changes, you can waste so much time and resources that it could cost you your entire business.

How do I react to failure?

The nature of business involves failure. The vast majority of small business fail in the first year or two for many reasons. For every successful product there are a box of failed products that either no one wanted or that just did not measure up to the competition.

It is not so much experiencing failure that is the most important part. It is what you do with that failure that can make all the difference. If you can emerge from failure smarter, wiser and stronger then that failure might actually be a success in the long term view. After all, what doesn't beat us makes us stronger. Learning from failures helps us stop making the same mistakes over and over and over again.

But if we are stubborn and always blame everyone else or refuse to admit defeat or deal with the failure, then we will continue to make the same mistakes over and over because we refused to accept responsibility for what went wrong.

The right approach is to accept the failure, determine what went wrong and why, make corrections and try again with a new approach. That is what helps make most businesses bigger successes than they would have normally been.

Am I comfortable dealing with other people?

With the possible exception of starting an online business, you are going to have to interact with customers, vendors, suppliers and other people on a daily basis. Even online businesses have a certain level of customer and vendor interaction. If you are not comfortable talking or interacting with people, it might be difficult for you to get what you want from the best source and at the best prices.

Can I negotiate effectively?

Business is one huge negotiation. We negotiate with suppliers and buyers and vendors for the best price or the best service. We negotiate with customers over price points and problem resolution. Very little in the business world is black and white. Instead it is a world of "gray" where both sides negotiate or bargain to get the most of what they want. If you find this difficult or troublesome, business ownership might not be for you.

Do I have a high level of confidence or self-esteem?

While not all businesses operate in a cut-throat or adversarial world, it is true that every so often things might not go smoothly or according to plan.

Not every business is successful right from the start and not every product becomes an instant hit with consumers. Because of this we need to have enough confidence to stick with a great idea or a good business even though things are not going so well.

We also need a healthy amount of self-esteem so we are not afraid to admit it when things do not go well due to a bad decision or an error in judgment. When a person is confident and has a healthy amount of self-esteem that are willing to accept blame and criticism when it is deserved and they will grow in the process. If we refuse to accept responsibility or fail to accept criticism we might stubbornly stay with an idea that is just bad and lose precious time and resources because of it.

Do I work well under pressure?

Some businesses are full of deadlines and decisions and other things that just have pressure associated with them. If you are not good making the tough decisions under pressure then you should either create a business where pressure is usually very low. But even then there will be pressure. If you honestly feel you can handle it, that's great. If you cannot handle the pressure it might be a good idea to have a partner who can handle it.

Am I comfortable taking calculated risks?

Starting ANY kind of business represents some kind of risk. It might be a few dollars for a domain name or a million dollars for a brick and mortar location full of inventory and equipment. Some people are made for this while some of us aren't. Which one are you?

It should also be said that there are good risks and bad risks. Being afraid to take a good calculated risk is one thing but refusing to take a really bad risk might just be very smart. Nerves and judgment help us separate the good risks from the bad ones. But if we search out the bad in everything we can often become paralyzed from taking any kind of action.

Am I comfortable making final decisions?

When you are the owner of your own business then everything stops with you. It's your business, your money, your products and your reputation. There is no one to hide behind and you must be comfortable making your own decisions. You can seek out the opinions of others but the final decisions will always be yours. Some of us are perfectly fine with this while others might struggle. Which one are you?

Do I have Basic Marketing or Sales Skills?

You don't have to become an expert on sales or marketing but you need to understand the fundamentals so that you can get things started until you can afford to hire other people or sub-contract the work out. Even then, you should know the basics so you can talk intelligently and not run the risk of being taken advantage of by others who realize you have no knowledge in that particular area.

Do I have Basic Business Skills?

Some people think that you get a great idea, produce a product or service and then sit back and watch the money roll in by the boat load. Unfortunately, that is far more dream than reality. The reality is that there is a lot more to running a business and you should have a working knowledge of how a business works.

If you don't know about how businesses work, I strongly suggest taking a course or seminar on business building before starting your own business. This can save you a lot of wasted time and money in the long run. Like in the previous question, it will also allow you to talk intelligently with other and avoid being taken advantage of or scammed.

Do I have the resources to start a business at this time?

One of the most common reasons for new businesses failing is that the owners do not have the resources required to sustain the business and their personal lives during the initial start-up period.

Depending on the type of business you are starting your business might not generate a profit for a year or more. Do you have money to tide you through that first year? Have you inquired within that industry how long it usually takes to get a new business into the profit stage? All of this information is critical when it comes to deciding when, or if, to start your new business.

I would strongly urge any person starting a business to get an accountant first. They will help you figure out what you might need by the way of money to get you through the start-up phase. You might not like what they tell you and this will cost you some money but it will save you a lot of money and heartache later.

What outside resources or contacts do have that can help me with my business?

I don't care who you are or how good you might be, you are going to need some help along the way.

Ask yourself what kind of resources you have available to you to call upon when that help is needed. These resources might be friends, local government programs or a local business incubator program designed to help new business owners.

Whatever resources you might have write them all down. It is not easy starting a new business and anything that will make it easier or more productive will help make your new business a success. You might even wish to consult with these people or programs before you launch the business. You can run your ideas through them and get their thoughts and input. It never hurts to get a second opinion or a different view on your business or idea for a business.

Am I financially responsible?

Especially at the very beginning, business require careful financial and asset planning in order to survive. If you are not good with money and bills this will spell disaster for your business. If your personal credit is in the tank and you cannot manage your own personal money, chances are you will either need a partner with a strong financial background or you will be in trouble.

Ask yourself if you have problems living on a budget or if you have a hard time managing your personal bills. Check your credit score to see if you have an excellent, good or poor credit rating.

If your credit rating is poor you will likely either have trouble getting credit accounts set up for your new business or you will be paying higher interest rates for those accounts.

If you are not currently financially responsible, you may wish to put off your business for a while until you can take a class in financial management and get used to handling money. This will also give you a chance to improve your credit score which might make it easier for you to get funding or credit accounts for your new business once you do get it started.

Am I physically capable of starting this type of business?

Some businesses are really easy and not at all physically demanding while others can be real back breakers. Take into consideration your age, overall physical condition and any health problems before starting your business. The last thing you want to have happen is to start the business, put in all the time and resources only to find out you cannot handle the workload or the tasks that need to be done.

If health or physical condition is a problem for you that does not mean you have to stop yourself from starting your own business.

You would just have to find a business that is less physically demanding so that you can better handle the workload.

For example, you might abandon a business that requires you to sell heavy products and instead create an online business where you have people drop ship the packages for you. It is much better to understand this now than after you invest time and money into a business you cannot physically handle.

What am I really good at?

Everyone has some things that they are really good at or better than most people. These are your core strengths and your business should be focused around these core strengths. These are also the things that you are not as likely to require help with as well so you would not have a problem handling tasks that required your core strengths.

Understanding the things you are really good at should help you decide if a business is a good fit for you as well. Most people who start a business create a business that deals with something they either know a lot about or have strong skills in that area. Since these are usually the things we enjoy or find interesting, it makes sense to develop a business that highlights or showcases your best skills.

What am I really bad at?

On the flip side of the spectrum, everyone has things that they are really bad at as well. Understanding what you are bad or not very good at is equally important. Understanding your weak points will allow you to determine what skills you should improve upon before starting your business. Other weak points could signal that you are just not cut out for the particular kind or type of business you are thinking about starting. It is better to find out now rather than later.

Once you understand your weak points, most of the time it is fairly easy to turn those weaknesses into strengths by taking a couple of courses, reading some books or just practicing something until you become good at it. You don't have to accept that you are bad at something and leave it at that. You can take steps to get better at whatever you want.

This is one area where you have to really be honest with yourself. No one likes to admit that they are bad at something and we will probably try to overstate our strengths and understate our weaknesses. So we convince ourselves we are better at something than we really are and that we are not as bad at other things as we really are.

No one else needs to be aware of our strengths and weaknesses. Only we need to know so that we can take action and make the right decisions when it comes to the business we are looking to start.

What criticisms have other people directed at me?

Sometimes others can let us know about possible problems or issues with how we do certain things. While we should never take what other people say as gospel or even as fact, if several people have made the same comments or expressed the same concerns, that could indicate a possible issue with a particular skills set or problem.

Think about what previous bosses or co-workers have told you about who well you do some things and also about any weak point or deficiencies that might be present as well. Sometimes we get so close to ourselves that we fail to notice what everyone else sees. Listening to what other people tell us can help us open our eyes to changes that need to be made.

What am I most praised or complimented about?

If you are constantly praised or commended about certain things, this would indicate a specialized or high skill level for a certain type of task.

Since our business should take advantage of those skill sets, understanding what we excel at is also a good thing.

When we get outside recognition it is usually because someone else sees something special within us. We might take it for granted or think it is nothing special but when other people notice, that could give us some insight into things we are really good at.

Why do I want to start my own business?

As we have already said, there are many reasons for wanting to start your own business. Understanding why you want to do this will help you decide if this is really a good idea and if your reasons are good reasons or just dreams. For example, if you want to start your own business because you want a stress-free job, that is just not reasonable. Any kind of business brings its own type of stress to the owner.

If you want to open your own business because you want to become a multi-billionaire and retire at the age of 35 you would have to ask yourself if that is reasonable as well. I am not saying it couldn't happen but it is not likely unless you happen to have that perfect idea or product that everyone needs yet no one has thought to develop yet. But it has happened.

Understanding your reasons and needs will help you decide on the right type of business and enable you to create the right business plan to create the best chance for success. As with everything in life, knowing where you want to go and why you want to get there helps you bring everything more into focus.

The Good

There are a lot of advantages to owning your own business. Many lives have been made better and happier through owning a business. But since many people do not understand what's involved in opening their own business, here are a list of the good points of owning your own business as compared to working for someone else:

Freedom

We have all seen those ads for get rich quick programs that tell you to "Fire Your Boss!" and those ads work because one thing most people hate about their job is that they have to be at work at a particular time and leave at a particular time. They also have to do what they are told when they are told to do it. Most people dislike that intensely.

When you own your own business, you can set your schedule pretty much however you want to as long as the needs of the business are taken care of. If you have employees, you can dictate when they work and create your own work hours to better suit your needs.

This can come in very handy when trying to attend school events or sporting events for your children or meeting family obligations. It also can come in handy when you have to take care of child care or when a child is sick and cannot go to school.

Regardless of the reason or need, having the ability to control your own work schedule is a major draw for people looking to step out of the corporate world and into their own business. Even though sometimes the number of work hours might actually be longer, the convenience outweighs the extra hours.

Stress Reduction

Some people experience a lot of stress in their careers or daily life and the ability to have more control over a larger part of their lives is more appealing to a lot of people. Owning their own business gives these people more control over what happens and the end result is that people experience less stress with this greater control.

Another stress related factor is that people who work for other people often feel powerless when it comes to what goes on and what decisions are made. Owning your own business means that you get to do things your way and that you have mostly total control over what happen and when it happens.

Wealth

Let's face it, when you work for someone else, your efforts and contribution earns you a salary while you go about making other people rich. Most of us would rather be the one getting all the money but when you work for someone else, that just doesn't happen.

Owning your own business means that after all expenses are paid what is left over is yours and yours alone (Well, except for taxes!) That means that if you put in long hours and create a profitable business that YOU will get the rewards not someone else. This can earn you a lot of money very quickly if you have the right idea or right product at the right time!

Pride of Accomplishment

When you build a successful business at some point you will look back and see what you create and there will be a sense of pride in what you have accomplished. Not everyone has the skills or abilities to create a successful business and you will have proven to the world that you are one of the few people to do so. The larger and more well-known your business becomes the more pride you will take in your accomplishment.

Recognition

Similar to taking pride in your business, the recognition you will receive from others for creating your successful business will feel good. It is a form of validation that can mean a lot for most people. It is one thing to feel pride in what you are doing or have done. But it is something else when other people step up and recognize you for your accomplishments

Control

When you own your own business, YOU have the most control over what happens moving forward. You can make all the decisions and you will have the most impact over where the business is headed and how business will be conducted. There will be no more frustration about having to do something a certain way because someone else decided that it should be done in that particular way.

When you own your own business YOU set the policies and YOU set the procedures. If you think something should be done a certain way you can do it that way and have your employees follow your way instead of someone else's way. This enables you to create a business that has your sense of tastes and you way of doing business. For a lot of people this is exactly what they need and want in their career.

Security

Whenever you work for someone else, your job is there only as long as someone in that company wants you there. Unless you have a contract or are a member of a union, your job can end whenever the company wants it to end. For most of us, that is a very unsettling concept. We all like to have security and most of us do not have it working for someone else.

When you own your own business, as long as the business remains profitable and can sustain paying you a salary, you will have a job and money will be coming in to pay the bills. Your security will not depend on the decisions of others or on business decisions made by others that might place the future of the business at risk.

The bottom line is that since the business will be following your direction and your leadership, that you will have a job and will be earning a salary as long as your skills and decisions continue to keep the business profitable and successful. When you stop and think about that, it is not a bad situation to find yourself in as compared to working for others.

Constant Change

Starting and operating your own business involves a lot of change both expected and unexpected.

One of the "fun" things many business owners enjoy is that no one day is like another. Something new or different is always standing in front of view.

Some people like this kind of environment and find it a real challenge while other hate it and like peace and quiet and the status quo. So while this might be a huge positive for some people it can also at the same time be a huge negative for others. Only you know which side of the fence you might find yourself on when it comes to change.

Options

With your own business, you control your destiny. You can change what you don't like and you can do pretty much whatever you want as long as you stay within the law and whatever rules and regulations that may apply to your business. No more having to put up with the direction from people you do not agree with or ever respect. You will control the shots and you control that part of your destiny.

The other part that is important as far as options are concerned is that you can sell your business at any time. You can sell all of part of it and move on with your life. You can build your business into a large business then sell it and retire. That is usually not something you can do working for others unless you earned a really large salary and had a lot of stock or stock options.

The thing is that people love options and choices and you get a lot more of them when you own your own business and have the control over that business that owners have. So if you want more options and more choices when it comes to your career and your future, consider owning your own business.

Tax Advantages

When you own a business, you are eligible for a whole other set of deductions that can help you keep more of the money that you earn from your business. These exemptions and deductions will allow you to shelter more money away for retirement and recoup certain expenses, or at least part of those expenses from taxes.

The larger your business the greater these savings are likely to be. If this sounds like it might be a good benefit for you, I urge you to select a qualified accountant while you are in the planning stages of starting your business so that they can advise you on the best way to create the business.

Making these kinds of decisions often requires knowledge that is far above what you and I currently have so it is worth the money to consult with a qualified accountant now rather than after in order to get the most benefit.

Examples of such savings might on for taking deductions for business use of your home, for vehicles leases and also deductions for company sponsored retirement plans.

The Bad

As with anything in life, what has positives or advantages also has some negatives as well. When it comes to owning your own business, there are some negatives to that as well. In some cases, some of the negative are the flips sides of the same issues that some might view as positives.

With all of that in mind, here are some of the possible negative of owning your own business that you should be aware of:

Time

Remember when we said that one of the best things about owning your own business is that you get to schedule yourself as you see fit and work when you want for as long as you wanted as long as the needs of the business were being met? Well, the flip side of that is that most small businesses require a lot more time especially during the start-up phase.

Many entrepreneurs and business owners look back and remember the long hours and sacrifices that they had to make to see their way through the tough early times of their business. They had to often work long hours with little or no compensation and were driven only by the belief that the rewards would come later after the business had become successful.

You need to be able to spend long hours at the beginning getting everything in place to create the type of business that your customers are going to want to purchase from. If you can make it through that time frame and create the business you want to create, you will be successful. But it is going to take a lot of time and effort to get to that place.

Money

When we think about business owners we usually think about being rich and making boatloads of money. While that can certainly become true in your future, you need to understand that most businesses do not open their doors and becoming profitable instantaneously. There is a time frame where most businesses do not make any profits or earn any money for their owners.

Depending on the business and industry that time frame might be close to instantly as in the introduction of a brand new and amazing product that everyone wants.

Or over a year before a business becomes known in the community or online and starts to attract a legitimate following.

During this time, sales might not be enough to generate any profits and probably will generate some kind of loss in the early stages.

It is important to realize and understand this because the business owner needs to have sufficient resources, or ways to access sufficient resources, to see them through this time frame. So this means that the business owner will not generate a salary for a long period of time but will also have to provide additional funds to keep the business going during the start-up period.

While your accountant can give you more accurate information, it is widely thought that the average business owner should be able to survive by not drawing a salary for the first year. That means having enough assets on hand to pay reasonable expenses during that time. If you do not have that kind of money, you either need to find a business that can be profitable sooner or invest in a similar, already established business that will generate income almost from day one.

Risk

When you work for a company and the company has a huge loss of millions of dollars, you still cash your paycheck and live your own life unless the loss is so great that you are laid off or otherwise let go. Losses do not directly effect you or your family. This is fair because cash windfalls that also come into the business do not go directly to you either.

When you own your own business, EVERYTRHING effects you. Profits and losses directly impact how much your business is worth and how much you can take out of the business in terms of salary and benefits. There is no isolation when you own the business! Everything always comes back to you!

Starting any kind of new business is risky. Over 90% of all new businesses fail for one reason or another so starting your own business is no sure thing. So you have to have a pretty good feeling about your ability to succeed before you even get started. Competition today is at an all-time high but so is opportunity for those who are able to take advantage of it.

Because of this it is usually a smart idea to never risk money that you cannot afford to lose. Do not cash out your retirement savings and mortgage your home on what you think is the next great idea. Always consider the worst and ask yourself if you can recover if you lose everything because that can happen.

Generally speaking, the older you are the less time you will have to recover from any kind of loss so be especially careful and do not gamble your future on a hunch that might never pay off. Always think of both the present and the future when making your decision.

Decision Making

This was listed as a positive as well because some people wish they could make all the tough decisions while others would be very happy to have someone always make them for them. When you own your own business the decisions are you because the money and the company are yours. If you are fortunate enough to be able to hire people to assist you, it might be possible to off-load some of the decisions to those individuals but even then, what they decide will impact you as well.

In short, if you like making important decisions and are able to make them quickly and decisively, often without all the information then this should not be an issue. But if you are of the type that has to always have the most information before making any kind of decision, it might be best to take on a partner who can help you in this regard.

Responsibility

This is an easy one. If you own your own business the responsibility for that business lies with you. Not a boss or manager or anyone else. It lies with you. If you can accept that then this will not be an issue. But if you have trouble accepting this kind of responsibility then you might want to consider the ownership route as far as the rest of your career is concerned.

One thing that holds many businesses back, and can even lead to their destruction, is the inability to make decisions quickly and accurately. The competition might be able to do things faster if you are not able to make calls quickly and get things done. For those people who have difficult making decisions this can be a significant negative.

Stress

Anytime you have a business you have stress. Stress is usually higher at the beginning when there are so many unknowns and so much appearing to be "up in the air" so to speak. Add to that the fear of whether or not the business will succeed and not knowing what is going to happen next can send stress levels significantly higher.

If there is a good side to stress it is that once the company starts becoming successful and the unknowns get less and less, stress usually goes down.

Plus, as time goes by and the business weathers through a tough time or two and emerges stronger or better, we become more at ease and there is less stress.

But no matter how good or great the business might be, there is still competition and there is still the need to constantly improve the business to keep customers happy and coming back. You can never say things are good enough and step back. You must always be engaged and always looking for ways to make your business better.

For many people, and most entrepreneurs, they thrive in this kind of environment and this is something they actually enjoy on a daily basis. But for others the constant change and the constant attention to detail can get stressful and overwhelming. If you enjoy the peace and quiet of the status quo, this can be a large negative.

Constant Change

We also mentioned this as a positive for some people but for some people constant change is considered a negative. Business owners face different challenges every single day. No day is like another and you never know who is going to walk through the door or be on the other end of the phone when you pick it up.

Some people feel this is exciting so for them it is not much of a negative. But for other people, constant change can be stressful and frustrating, you really need to understand the type of person you are and how you are likely to react to this kind of environment.

Legal Exposure

We are not lawyers and the intention here is not to give you specific legal advice but only to inform you that owning your business can have a considerable legal impact on your personal life as well.

Any problems or damage claims coming from your business can wind up leaving you personally liable for damages unless you have taken specific steps to isolate your personal possessions and assets from your business. I urge everyone thinking about starting their own business to contact a good lawyer familiar with business assets and liability to advise you on the best way for you to set up your new company. A few dollars spent now could very well save you millions later!

Please understand that the intent of this chapter was not to scare you away from starting your own business. But we also do not want you thinking that owning your own business is all fun and games either. Anytime money and careers are involved there are upsides and downsides. To consider only the upsides is both foolish and dangerous.

So please understand both the good and the bad when it comes to owning your own business and use that information to decide whether this is something you really want to become involved with. Be honest with yourself and possibly even get the opinions of a few close friends as well. Then, if you still think it is a great idea you are ready to go.

If you do not think it is a good idea ask yourself what bothers you about it and then take steps to address your concerns. You might find out that this might not be a good idea right now but probably would be a better idea a year or more from now when you are better prepared to do things right.

Love What You Do
& Do What You Love

While I cannot tell you what kind of business to open or what types of products or services to offer, I would like to impact one little bit of advice that might make the world of difference to you and your business. Sometimes it can mean the difference between success and failure of the business!

I strongly urge you to create your business about something that you love or are passionate about. The reason for doing this is three-fold.

First, this business is going to occupy a great deal of your time so it just makes sense that you should be doing something you love or are very good at. If you have to spend your time doing something that you hate or have no interest in you will be in store for a lot of tedious work in the months and years ahead.

Second, doing something we love or are passionate about makes it a lot easier to put in the time required to make your business the very best it can be. It will make building your business enjoyable and exciting and not make it seem like work at all. This should be one of your prime objectives.

For me personally, I love writing and website design. There have been many of times when I have starting something early in the morning and then looked at my watch for the first time and saw it was late in the afternoon! That is what you are looking for. You want to find something that you love so much that the time just flies by as you do the things necessary to create the best business you are capable of.

Third, no matter how much you love something there will always be a part of the business which might not be all that exciting. Perhaps it's the details or one aspect of some process that you don't enjoy. That's perfectly fine. We can't like everything or be good at everything. But the more we enjoy as part of the entire business, the more likely we will stick to what needs to be done and see if through to completion.

The human brain is a wondrous thing but there are parts of it that sometimes get in our way.

One of these things is that our brains want us to do more of the things we enjoy and less of what we don't enjoy. It will create reasons for us to stop doing certain things while at the same time making it easier to do other things for longer periods of time. The key is to help our brain react in ways that will help us achieve more in less time with greater results.

By creating our business around something we love or enjoy, we are telling our brains that this is something that makes us happy. Our brains in turn will help us stay more motivated and engaged for longer periods of time. We will be able to spend more time designing the best possible product or the best performing website. We will write better sales copy and create better looking advertisements. It's just all part of the process.

I also would urge you not to go into business strictly because it will make you more money. While money is a terrific motivator, it is a short term motivator not a long-term one. After a while money will stop motivating you and then you might find yourself spending long hours working on something you don't enjoy for reasons that no longer might apply.

For those of you who disagree with the fact that money only motivates us for a short period of time, think about this for a moment:

How many times have you be happy to get a raise and had then improved your performance at work. But then after you cashed a few of those larger checks, the same things that bothered or frustrated you in the past came back. The still bothered you because the added money only mattered to you until you got used to it. The other things were always there, the money just made you ignore them for a little while.

That's not to say that money should not be a consideration because it is important. After all, you should not go into business if the type of business you want to open has no chance of generating a profit for you. Your business needs to have a market segment strong enough to support the business but it should not be the only motivator behind you going into business.

Just remember that this is your life we are talking about and your business will soon occupy a great deal of your time and thoughts. Would you agree that it is better to spend all that time and all those thoughts on something that makes you smile and allows you to be happy?

If you can achieve that, you have already made your business into a real success!

Choosing the Type of Business

Now that we have got all the preliminary things out of the way and you have finally realized that you really do have what it takes to start your own business we come to the first decision we have to make. That is exactly what type of business are we going to create.

While there are many different types of business we can go about creating, for our purposes we are going to deal with just two broad types to start off with and then we will go from there. The two major types we are going to consider at this point are your standard storefront or "brick and mortar" stores and online or "web-based" stores.

What kind of store you should open is largely going to depend on the resources you have behind you and the type of products or services that you intend to sell. Very often just asking yourself those two questions will give you the answer that you will need.

Online or Web-Based Stores

It used to be that if you wanted to start your own business selling any kind of product you either had to open a real storefront or sell via mail order. In those days mail order was not only tedious and slow but also had kind of a "cheesy" reputation of selling poor quality or over-hyped products.

But with the advent and arrival of the internet, opening up an online business is as easy as grabbing the right domain name, designing a website and getting traffic to go to it. This has made starting your own business something just about anyone with even the smallest amount of resources can easily do.

One of the most endearing qualities of an online business is that you can start one for less than $20! For less than $20 you can get a domain name for a year and a hosting package that will enable you site to be seen on the internet. I'm not sure there is anyone out there that wants to start their own business that doesn't have $20 to their name to start their business.

Another advantage when it comes to online businesses is that the internet creates a somewhat level playing field when it comes to competing for customers.

People will see only what your website allows them to see so if you can design a nice looking professional website they will not realize that they are dealing with a small business operating out of a small bedroom in your parent's house or a multi-million dollar Fortune 500 company! Of course this ease of operation makes it easier for everyone to start their own business so competition is higher as well.

On-line businesses also have the advantage of having extremely low overhead. Many businesses are run out of the family home and have no need for a storefront and rent or insurance. They usually have fewer employees as well. In fact, it is possible to design a web-based business that is totally automated that requires no interaction between the business and the customer unless a problem arises!

The key to online business success is getting enough people to see your website. But not just anyone but the people who are already known to have an interest or need for the products or services that you sell. This kind of "traffic" is known as "targeted" traffic. Targeted traffic is more expensive but converts into actual buyers at a much higher percentage that untargeted traffic.

One interesting thing about online businesses is that they are not limited to a small geographical area like brick and mortar stores are.

Since you are buying products through your credit card or online payment service and getting them shipped to you, it makes little difference where the selling company is located. So your "little" on-line business can sell its products and services all over the world.

If you are looking to start a business on a shoestring budget, or if you are just trying to find a way to see if you are really cut out for operating your own business, then perhaps starting an online business and seeing how well you are suited for running a business might be the best option for you. In fact, some people start an online business to gauge interest in the product and to see if money can be made selling it. Then they use the money they generated from their on-line business and open up a brick and mortar store.

What kinds of products and services lend themselves well to on-line sales? It used to be that only small and easy to ship products were sold on-line because the shipping costs were so high. But with shipping prices coming down, just about any product can now be purchased on-line. So an on-line presence should at least be considered whenever you are thinking about starting a business.

Services such as carpet cleaning and lawn services can be marketed online but also need to be supported on a local basis as well. These types of business usually operate best as "hybrid" business which will be discussed a bit later.

"Brick & Mortar" Stores

Brick and mortar stores are what we see in our town or neighborhood. These are the places we go to physically buy products and services in person. Grocery stores, pharmacies and restaurants are perfect examples of brick and mortar stores. They have been around for thousands of years and these are the places we go when we need something right now or when we need to physically see and touch the product before we buy.

Brick and mortar storefronts are usually very expensive to create and can sometimes set the business owner back a million dollars or more before the doors are even opened! So this can severely limit the number of people that are financially able to open this type of store. Plus, the month to month expenses in employees, utilities, taxes and insurance can also get to be very substantial as well.

Because of this there is much more risk involved in a brick and mortar store. It is one thing to risk $50 to set up an internet website and another to invest a few hundred thousand dollars in a brick and mortar store.

If your internet business tanks you are out $50 so that's not a big deal. But if that brick and mortar store tanks, you could spend a lifetime earning that lost money back. So needless to say, if you are contemplating opening a brick and mortar store you should be doing a lot more market and consumer analysis to make sure a local market exists for your products and services before you open the doors. You also need to carefully evaluate your competition to make sure a new and unknown business will be able to crack though the market and be able to exist with the already established players in the market.

Hybrid Stores

Hybrid stores are stores that combine a brick and mortar store with an online presence as well. This is a common business model today where so many people search online first and then follow-up with brick and mortar listings they find during their online searches. In this business model an online search takes the customer to a brick and mortar address where the customer will already know the product is stocked and available for purchase.

This model works best because most consumers are at least partially lazy and instead of driving around looking for what they want they will first search through their keyboard to save them time, money and wasted gas. With the cost of gas so high you cannot blame people for doing their research online instead of on the road.

Which is the Best Option for You?

Of course you are the best one to decide which avenue or approach you would like to take when it comes to your business. Plus, the type of business you are interested in will often dictate which type of business model you should use. In those cases the decision will often be made for you.

For example, if you are a gourmet cook and want to open your own restaurant, then obviously you would need a brick and mortar business location where people can actually go to sit down and eat. An online business would not be a good fit unless your gourmet food products can be packaged and shipped and still retain their flavor and appeal.

The same might be said for automotive repair services or repair services for any item that is too bulky or inconvenient to ship. But today shipping is getting easier and easier and is faster now as well. You just need to factor in shipping costs into your business model when setting competitive price points.

For most small business owners, the online model is by far the cheapest and less risky alternative. As I stated before, and will talk in depth about later on, you can start an online business for less than $50 so even if your business for some reason became an instant or total failure, you would only be out a bit of time and just $50. Almost anyone can withstand that kind of loss.

If you are selling products that are able to be easily shipped you might want to start out as an online business to gauge interest in your products before investing a lot of money in an actual retail location. The only downside is that competitors might see your success and notice your product line and beat you to a retail location but if you are truly successful that is going to happen anyway.

If you do not have access to the funds to open a retail business then the answer has been made for you and perhaps you either start out online until you get the funds needed or you put off the business for a while until you can either save or get access to the funds you need. After all, the retail world does require a lot of upfront money in build costs and inventory.

If that is the route you really believe you should go, and if you have the access to the funds that you will need to not only start the business but carry you through the initial start-up phase before your business starts turning a profit, there is one step I must insist that you take to safeguard your future.

That step is to meet with your accountant so he or she can advise you on whether you have enough funds and are capable of taking those funds and using them to start your own business. Emptying your 401K and taking out a mortgage on your home at age 59 to pursue a dream is not a responsible thing to do and your accountant will tell you that. Go to your accountant and listen to what he or she says. Do not think you know better or that they are wrong. You are paying them for their opinion so you might as well listen to them.

Choosing & Protecting Your Name

Whenever you go into business the name you choose is very important. For online businesses the name is how people are going to search for your business online. For a retail business, your name will appear in phone books and other publications as well as local online search results. So you want the name of your business to be easy to remember yet also letting the public know what type of business it is.

Some people like to go the generic route and choose a broad name that will allow them to sell anything. If your business is a business that sells a wide variety of products that might work for you. But if your business centers on a specific type of product, choose a name that will reflect what you sell. This makes it easier for people to understand what you sell as well as remembering your name when it becomes time to buy.

For example, you might call your business "Dave's" and that might be a great name for a restaurant or Pub but people who are looking for products might not know what the heck Dave is selling! So you might consider changing the name to "Dave's Antiques" or "Dave's Music" or something like that. Even if you do own a restaurant you might use "Dave's Ribs" or Dave's English Pub" to help paint a picture in the mind of the prospective customer.

Here are some things you should consider when choosing your business name:

It Should Paint a Picture

As we just stated, your name should create a picture or image in the mind of the customer and let them know they are likely to find what they are looking for at your store. People do not like to waste time looking to see if a store carries the products they need. They want to know that upfront and a descriptive name will help them know what you are selling.

Keep it Short

Your name should be short and sweet so people can easily remember it. When it comes to an online business, your domain name should be your business name or something really close if your exact name is already taken.

In fact, I suggest getting your domain name first and choose your business name by what is still available. This will help people find you on the internet.

Even then, the domain name should be short so it is easy for people to remember and type into their browser. The other reason for keeping it short is that the less a person has to type the less of a chance there will be for them to make mistakes. This means a much better chance of them actually getting to your website and not someone else's.

Make it Easy to Remember

If you want people to remember your name you have to pick a name that is easy for people to remember. "Dave's Ribs" is short and to the point. It is descriptive and easy to remember. "Dave's Mouthwatering BBQ Foods" is longer and harder to remember. Which one do you think you would remember easier?

Do Not Duplicate

The problem with some simple names is that they are already in use by other businesses. Now while that doesn't mean you cannot use the same name, it does create confusion. Plus, if you try and use the same name as a well-known or established business, you could be getting a call from their lawyers very shortly.

We want the name to be appropriate for our business and we do not want to cause any confusion in the minds of our customers. So pick a name that adequately describes your business but is also not in use in your area today. After all, you would not like it if someone used your business name to steal away customers so don't try the same thing yourself with other people's business names.

Protecting Your Name

Once you have decided on your business name, you need to take a few basic steps to protect that name against other people using it. Fortunately that is very easy to do for both online business and brick and mortar businesses.

Though the actual process might vary depending on where you live or do business, the following processes are usually what new business owners need to follow to register their new business name:

On-Line Businesses

Protecting or registering an online domain name is actually done for you once you pay for the domain name. You pick out the name you want and go to the registrar company and search for that name. If no one is using that name you can purchase that domain for a yearly fee.

Once you purchase that particular domain name no one else can use it or register it. They can register a name that is very close but they cannot duplicate your exact name.

For example if you registered the domain "davesribs.com" no one else could register that domain name. But they could register "davesribs.info" or "davesribs.biz" or any of the other domain extensions. They could also register "davesribz.com" because they use a "z" instead of an "s" in the name.

So if there are any variations of the name, or if you want to register the same name under any other domain extensions, make sure you do that all at once to protect the value of your name. The cost will be different for each domain extension so be careful and choose wisely to make sure you do not waste money registering not needed domains.

Once you register a domain name you own it until the registration period is up. You will always be reminded and will have a certain time frame during which you can renew it. After that time period if your do not renew your domain name anyone can step in and register it.

For this reason I would suggest that once your business has been established and appears to be successful that you go ahead and register it for 5 or 10 years to protect that name and your brand. It almost always turns out to be less expensive that way as well because domain costs rise every couple of years anyway.

Brick & Mortar Businesses

Brick and Mortar stores require a different process and more work to register a business name. You will usually have to go to a local government office, do a name search to make sure no one else is using that name. Then if the name is not used you can fill out an application, pay a registration fee, and register that name in your state. You can usually complete this all in the same day.

The actual process may vary in your country or state so be sure to check with local authorities to find out what you must do to register your business in your area. Be sure to follow the directions completely and properly to save time and money.

Even after registering you might still find businesses using your name or similar names so be sure to protect your business with a unique name that will showcase your brand and protect it from others.

For example you might have several nail salons throughout your State that are called "Mary's Nail Salon" But chances are they are all located in different towns. They will not usually allow two businesses to share the same name if they are located in the same town. But to avoid confusion, try and come up with a short name that is not likely to be found elsewhere. Your goal is to avoid confusion with other businesses with the same name.

Business Names & Financial Institutions

Registering a business name might be required even for online businesses as well because if you want to open accounts at your bank to cash payments or checks made out to your business they will usually want to see proof of business and that is usually found in your business name registration paperwork.

On yet another level, registering a business name will also be mandatory if you create your business as a corporation or partnership. For tax purposes you will need to register as well. Your accountant can provide you with guidance on this aspect of registering the business.

Once you register your name it will be "connected" to you until you decide to shut the business down.

Even if you do not do any business throughout the year you might still have to file state business tax forms as long as the name is active. Again your accountant can inform you of all that is needed on a yearly or quarterly basis.

Once you have decided on a name and registered it, you need to protect that name by making sure you treat your customer's right and develop a good reputation. You also need to keep watch that no one else copies your name and gives your business a bad name by cheating their customers and having them think you are somehow connected to their business.

Once your business has become known in the industry or your community you might find other business trying deceitful or underhanded ways to steal your customers or ruin your brand name. Always be on the alert for this type of behavior and report it to your lawyer and the authorities if you see someone is going after your business.

Establishing Goals
& Objectives
(Your Business Plan)

I can already hear the groans readers are making when they read the title of this chapter and see that we are asking them to establish goals and objectives and use those goals and objectives to create a business plan. People groan and moan about this because they do not see the value in this exercise. They see it as a massive waste of time but they are 1,000% dead wrong.

It is just not possible to get where you are going in the shortest period of time if you don't know your destination before-hand. Even though you might eventually get there you will take a lot more time and drive a lot more wasted miles to get to the same destination. This is just not a smart use of time and/or resources.

Some people want to know what the difference is between a goal, dream or objective.

The easiest way to explain the difference is by saying that a goal is a dream with a timeline attached to it. If you do not have a deadline or time frame attached to something, it is just a dream. You still want to achieve something or accomplish something but you have no idea when or how this is going to happen.

Listen, when it comes to work I hate goals just as much as everyone else does. But despite that feeling towards goals I also understand that nothing keeps us focused and on track better than a well thought out and designed goal. Nothing also gives us a better vantage point of knowing where we stand than a well-designed goal either. So like them or not, we must agree that we need goals to help us make our business a success.

In order for goals to be able to help us, they must be created in the proper manner and contain some very important characteristics. So with that in mind, follow this approach when creating your goals:

Your goals must be S.M.A.R.T. That means they must be:

Specific – the goal must be well defined with specific targets

Measureable – there has to be accurate and factual ways of measuring progress.

Achievable – every goal needs to be able to be achieved through a normal effort.

Realistic – goals must be reasonable both in time frame and expectations

Timely – you cannot have a goal without a time frame for achieving the goal.

Though this is an over simplification of the goal setting process, goals give us the ability to measure progress against expectations and allow us to see whether we are moving in the right direction or the wrong direction. It also allows us to measure progress versus time to make sure we remain on track to obtain our objectives within a certain period of time.

There is another saying that goes something like "What gets measured gets done." And this refers to once a goal is given to someone they feel an obligation or pressure to reach or exceed that goal. It is not enough to just say I am going to achieve something. When you do that you are opening up a host of generalities that does little or nothing to help you get or stay on track.

But when you tell yourself that you are going to achieve something within a certain time frame or by a certain date, that makes the statement turn into a goal and that goals gives you something to aim or shoot for. It gives you something to compare yourself against as well. When you add a time frame, magic happens.

If you just tell yourself you are going to get better, you can look at yourself 10 years from now and see that you got better. But di that really help you or your business?

But if you told yourself you were going to improve sales by 100% within 6 months, and you looked 3 months later and saw that sales were still flat, you would know you had some serious work to do in the next 3 months.

Goals just allow you to get a plan in place, help you get started and also help stay on track and help you get back on track when you fall off.

Your Business Plan

Your business plan is where you take your goals and list them as your objectives. Then you take each objective and figure out what needs to be done to hit that objective within the required time frame. In other words, this is where you turn your goals into action items designed to get you where you want to be.

As you craft your plan, there will usually be several parts of your plan with each running at the same time or concurrently. Each item will have several steps and a logical order in which those steps need to be performed in order to get you to your goals in an orderly and efficient manner.

In other words, there are certain things that have to be done before other things can be done. By taking time to create a plan we can make sure all the first steps are completed so we can get to the second steps and so on.

This helps save time and resources while at the same time allowing you to move forward a lot faster and with much less stress and fewer delays.

As we assign time frames to each step we can then refer back to our plans every week or every month and see where we are as opposed to where we should be. If we are ahead of schedule that's great! But if we are behind schedule we can decide what needs to be changed or what has to be done to get ourselves back on schedule.

This is important because goals and time frames help us stay on track and even more important, help us identify potential problems much faster which enables us to get back on track much faster. This helps us save time, money and resources. It also helps keep problems smaller and reduces the effects of those problems at the same time. Goals and business plans just enable us to become and stay more focused and more responsive moving forward.

Another important thing that a business plan does is remind everyone of what we need to do and what our objectives are. The more people who are involved in a business the more important a master business plan will become.

But even if you are a one person business, you need to remind yourself from time to time about where you are versus where you wanted to be. This is the only way for you to make sure you continue to make the progress you need to create the business you want and to accomplish all of this on time.

The Need for Organization

Behind the success of every business of any size lies an underlying framework or organization. This means that the structure of the business and how certain things are done has a certain amount of processes and procedures that dictate how certain things are done throughout the business. This is important because in order for any business to be successful, there has to be a common approach to business and customer care. We cannot just "wing it" when situations arise every day.

Organization means that there are plan in place for most of the common situations and procedures contained within the business. These are important because there will always be certain things that have to be done and certain practices that have to be followed. We also need this type of framework to create a uniform customer experience regardless of who the customer might talk to at any given time.

Think about the number of things that need to happen for any business to stay in business and be responsive to their customers. There are bills to be paid, orders to be shipped, follow-ups to customers and vendors, advertisement to be placed, products to be developed of evaluated and customer disputes or complaints that need to be addressed. Skip any of these and the damage to the business could be severe.

In the operation of any business there needs to be a certain order as to what gets done when so everything proceeds in an orderly manner. For example, advertising must be placed before certain deadlines and bills need to be paid on time to avoid finance charges and other similar items.

For online business domains must be monitored, sites checked for viruses and malware and orders checked to make sure payments were credited to the proper accounts and that those accounts are still secure. These are just a few of the things that need to be taken care of on a regular basis.

It is very easy to forget about these things as they run silently in the background of the business and until they cause a problem you just take them for granted. But if you do not check on these things, problems can go unnoticed and the result can be a serious loss of income and damage to your business.

If you are an organized person then all of this comes as no surprise to you. After all you are taking care of the same little things in your everyday life. So the transition to doing the same thing in your business will come easy to you. You just carry over the same habits and approach to your business.

But if you are the type of person whose personal life is all over the place and you have no idea what account does what or if you have not balanced a check book or looked at your account balances for 3 years, then you could be in trouble. If you look around your apartment and see stuff all over the place and you have no idea when bills are due or when you last checked your finances, you could be in real trouble if you started your own business. While this is not an insurmountable problem it is one that you need to be aware of before starting your business.

Because organization is so important I suggest that you create a monthly calendar that lists every deadline or day where a certain action item is to be completed by. If a bill is due on the 21st of every month, place that on your monthly calendar. That way you will always have a gentle reminder of what needs to be done so nothing falls through the cracks.

You should also have a yearly calendar as well to remind you of the things that should be done throughout the year as well. That might be the changing of passwords every six months, complete site maintenance 2 or 3 times a year and the checking of all online and other accounts to make sure there is no suspicious activity on any of them. Then, you just follow your established calendar to make sure everything is taken care of that needs to be taken care of.

Then the next step should sitting down and designing rules and procedures for the various tasks that you are going to encounter on a regular basis. This would include how to handle customer complaints and refunds, how to introduce new products on your website, how to design advertising materials, and how to process customer information so that it is captured on a customer mailing list. This is only a small sampling of what you might need to create processes and procedures for.

Doing this in the beginning helps establish a set pattern for how business is going to be done moving forward. As you add employees, having all of this organizational structure in place will help everyone do things in pretty much the same manner. As the company grows and more people are added there will likely be more levels of management as well. The larger the company the more organization needs to play a significant role in how things are done.

But the most important aspect of the business that needs the most amount of organization should be on the financial or fiscal side of the business. You are going to need to make 100% sure that all bills and taxes are paid in the correct amounts and at or before they are due. This will help you avoid penalties and damage to you or your business' credit rating.

Plus, you are going to need to organize your books so that you insure that all orders are being paid for and all expenses are documented and paid as well. This is important because there will always be the customer or two who will try and skate around the system and scam you. The might demand a refund without ever buying the product in the first place. Because of this all purchases and refunds need to be entered into the system immediately so everyone has the most up to date information available when it comes to handling customer issues.

You are also going to have to organize every account that your business has to make sure no one has stolen funds or otherwise hacked in your account. This is fast becoming a very common and dangerous activity. You might think that no one will bother your business because it is very small and not earning much money, especially at the very beginning.

But if you continue with that belief you will soon be at the mercy of a hacker. I personally had a site that generated extremely little business because it had not yet been developed but one day we attempted to log into it and were frozen out and when you logged into the site you saw a pirate banner with a hackers group name on it! If you never check, you will never be aware that anyone has hacked your site!

The real danger, especially with online businesses that can be made completely automated, is not to forget to check on things every so often to make sure that sales are still being made and credited and that nothing needs to be addressed. You want to make sure names are being added to your customer mailing list and that goods and order are being processed properly and sent out on time.

Organization is not glamorous and it is not always easy. But the great thing about organizing your business is that after you are done it makes managing and operating your business properly much easier. In the long run it will save you time and energy and help you protect your business and all your assets. It is something that really isn't an option. There is little room in a successful business for disorganization and confusion.

What Should I Sell? (What Makes a Great Product?)

No matter what kind or type of business you are thinking about starting or have already started, you are going to need something to sell. You are going to need something for customer to purchase and to earn money to help sustain your business. Your product is going to be either a physical product, a service, or knowledge and information. All products will be in one or more of those 3 groups.

Now just because you have a product does not mean that your business is automatically going to be success and that profits are going to start rolling in. In order for a product to be a good seller, it must have a few important characteristics to make it desirable to your customers so they will spend their hard earned money on it.

In order to be success a product must have one or more of the following 10 characteristics:

It Must Address a Need

In order for a product to be successful it needs to address or fulfill some kind of need. Naturally the more urgent the need the more valuable or desirable the product is going to be. So a great product would be one that helps a customer address an important need in his or her life.

For example, a car addresses the need for transportation. A pair of pant addresses fashion and clothing needs. Tools address repair and building needs. Medicine and vitamins address health needs. The more important the need, the more the customer is likely to want the product.

If there is an urgent yet common need that has not been addressed by any product as yet and you can develop that product, you might very well have a huge winner in your hands!

It Must Solve a Problem

Life is full of problems and people are always looking for anything to help them solve those problems and make them go away. The more serious or urgent the problem might be, the more people are going to want any product that helps them with their problems.

Weight loss books help people lose weight. Information books give people instruction on how to solve a problem or accomplish a certain task.

Medicines can help relieve symptoms or cure medical problems. House cleaning services help people keep their houses clean when they don't have the time to do it themselves.

The more severe and widespread the problem might be the more people are going to want your product and pay your price. A bottle of water in the store might be worth a dollar but that same bottle of water in the desert when it is 112 degrees out and someone is dying of thirst will be worth a lot more!

It Should Make Life Easier

This should not come as a surprise to anyone but people love products that make any part of life easier for them. If your product can make a common task or situation easier to handle, people are going to want it and they will be more than willing to pay for it.

In fact, the "quick and easy" group of products has been shown to be the hottest sellers among all age groups! So if you can develop or get a product to see that makes losing weight easier or allows you to cut the lawn or vacuum the pool much faster, you should do very well!

If your product does offer ease and swiftness as a benefit make sure you include this in all of your marketing materials.

This is a powerful selling point and marketing tool to increase sales and profits.

It Should Make Life More Enjoyable

Everyone likes to have fun and everyone wants their lives to be more enjoyable. So if your product can give someone more fun or make them smile more and just become happier, there is a great value in that.

There are a ton of products out there that you might think were stupid but are making their sellers insanely rich! Always keep an eye out for products that make people laugh or smile. There is a huge market for these kinds of products.

It Should Make Someone Better or More Desirable

If you have a product that makes anyone look better, appear more desirable or just makes someone better in any way, you have a winner on your hands! And if that product makes it easier for people to attract members of the opposite sex, you could become the next millionaire.

People want any product that makes them appear better than what they really are. Cosmetics are a prime example of this. Billions of dollars are spent every year on products to make people appear younger and better looking than they are naturally.

It Should Be Appropriately Priced

There should be an appropriate relationship between what the product is, what it can do for you and what the cost of the product sells for. Prices set too high can drive buyers away while prices too low might lead people to think that the overall quality of the product is very poor.

Your products selling price should be based on not just what it costs to make but what benefits the product will bring to the customer. We also need to take into consideration the "perceived value" in the eyes of the customer. The "perceived value" is what the customer thinks your product is worth. As long as you come in at or slightly under the customers "perceived value" you should do well.

It Should Appeal to a LOT of People

Even though you might have the best product in the world not everyone is going to buy it from you. Not everyone needs the same product or likes the same things. Not everyone has the same needs or experiences the same problems either. So in order to have the best and most success, your product should be designed to address the largest and most diversified audience.

You might have a choice of two products to sell. One product solve the problem of people with a certain type of foot finding comfortable shoes. That might effect 1 million people in the world today. Not too shabby but not everyone with that problem is going to hear about your product let alone buy one. So your sales would be limited.

But if you had a product that made it super easy for people to lose weight quickly and easier and in a healthy manner, there would likely be tens, or hundreds, of millions or people clamoring for such a product. The audience would be much larger and therefore you would make a lot more sales because you would have a lot more customers.

It should be Different or Unique

If your product is exactly like someone else's, why would people buy yours over someone else's? It is likely that they wouldn't. In order for a new product to sell well it needs to be unique in some manner. It should have more features, do what it is intended to do better or faster and maybe even needs to be priced lower.

Whatever these differences might be they MUST be there or your product will just sit there on the shelf. So when you are designing a new product, or evaluating a product that you are thinking about selling, always ask yourself what makes this product better or different than anything else on the market today?

If the answer is that there is nothing different about it, pass on that product and look for something else.

It should be Multi-Functional

The best products are those products that can do more than one task or products that can replace several different product with just the one new product. For some people space is at a premium so if they can find something that replaces several other things they can save space and add convenience at the same time.

Look at our current cell phone which are perfect examples of one device handling several functions. With the one small device you can use it as a cell phone, book reader, e-mail device, wake-up timer, camera video game player, music player, movie player and lord knows how many other things you can use it for with the multitude of apps that are available for it.

Is it a wonder that devices like the IPAD have become so popular as well? They can do almost unlimited things as well with the same apps that we can get for our phone. For the ultimate in convenience IPAD and other E-Book readers allow you to take hundreds of books with you in less space than it would take to fit one into your suitcase or carry-on.

So think multi-functional and you'll be thinking sales as well!

It Should Be Simple & Easy to Use or Operate

If your product has a 4,237 page user manual, it might do an amazing job at a lot of things but it will also turn off a lot of potential buyers because it is too complicated. The best products are the ones that are easy to learn and mostly intuitive. By that we mean that most people can just pick it up and figure it out easily without needing a manual.

The easier you can make something to use the more people will like it and purchase it. Simple is usually best unless your product caters to a professional level customer with advanced product or industry knowledge. For those customers, performance and features are more important than ease of use. But since there are more customers with normal level skills, the easier to operate, the better.

So how do you think your product matches up to these 10 characteristics? The more of these items your products have, the more popular they will be. To get a better overall idea of where your product matches up, use this simple chart:

Hits all 10 items perfectly = Start looking at houses on Maui! Ka-Ching!

Hits 8 or 9items = You've got a real winner here!

Hits 6 to 8 items = You should do well with this product

Hits 4 to 6 items = Can do well with some work. Most products are here.

Hits 2 to 4 items = Has potential but must strongly hit those 2-4 items

Hits 0 to 2 items = A Crapshoot but still might work.

Hits 0 items =   Why would anyone buy this product????

Are there going to be exceptions to these rules? Of course, but those are the exception to the rules and a smart business owner will not build their business around products that do not have a strong market appeal. But that is not to say that there is no room for the odd product in your business.

I would suggest that a new business owner have several products that hit as many of the listed characteristics as possible. You want to start out with the very best products you possibly can because you are not just trying to sell products but also to build your business and strengthen your brand at the same time.

In the very beginning people are not going to know you or your business so the product has to capture their attention and thoughts. You do not as yet have a brand to attract people so it is all up to the product.

Having a dynamite product that really gets the attention of consumers is very important to the new business. So focus on these products at the very beginning until you get known in the industry or in your marketplace.

Once you have an established and respected line or group of products that are bringing people to your website or into your stores, then you can introduce one of the weaker or unknown products to see how they might sell in your business. This is the best approach because the stronger products are still bringing people in and creating sales which help pay the bills. But these same people are also seeing the other products and might purchase them as well leading to more sales and larger sales.

You might even see one of the product you thought was a risk really take off and become a popular seller! When this happens that's great! But you should never invest a lot of money or build a business around a weak product hoping it will catch on. There is just too much to lose for the new business owner.

That being said, we mentioned that you can set up an online business for under $50 and if you feel that one of the weaker product just might catch on with the public, there is nothing to say that you cannot create a quick website, grab a domain name and see what happens. Sales might explode or they might tank. But if all you invested were a few hour's time and $50, the loss would not be that great and the upside might just make it all worthwhile.

Investigating the Market

Before you invest a lot of time and money in your new business, spend a while doing a bit of market research to see if there is a market for your products and if there is, what kind of competition you might find yourself up against. This will help you decide if this is a good idea or if you should look for something else to start a business around.

When choosing a market you have to deal with a bit of unorthodox thinking. Conventional wisdom might tell you that if there are a lot of people already selling your product that this would be a bad business because there was so much competition. And they would have a valid point. Sometimes you might find yourself going up against a few retail giants which might prove very difficult for you.

That same line of thinking would also believe that if there was no one selling your particular product then you would have the market all to yourself and that it would be easier for you to get your product seen and noticed by customers. After all, if someone wanted your product and you were the only one selling it, you are likely to get the sale!

So all of this really seems to make sense and there is a certain logic about it. But now let me tell you why that line of reasoning might be very flawed.

Let's say your business is called "Peter's Amazing Garlic Roasted Avocado Balls" and you look around your local area and see that no one is selling garlic roasted avocado balls. Your search online and see that no one is selling them online either! So that means that the entire market is wide open to your garlic roasted avocado balls! You've cornered the market and everyone who wants them will have to buy them from you!

But here's why this line of logic is flawed:

If there is no one selling them locally or online, that means no one is buying them either. So there is no established market for your garlic roasted avocado balls. Granted there might be a ton of people who might like them and might buy them if you went into business but you will never know until you invest the time and money into your business and actually put them up for sale.

When there is no pre-existing market then you are going to have to create a market from scratch and that can be very time consuming and extremely expensive. Larger and more established businesses might be able to do that but for someone just starting off, that can be very rough.

On the other hand, if the competition for your product is very high, that tells you that there is already a large market for your products. If there are a lot of people already selling garlic roasted avocado balls you have a pretty good idea that there are a lot of people buying them. People who are successful offer products that people want. They look for trends and they look for what is selling well at the moment.

Then other people will come into the market selling the same products to get a piece of what was a lucrative market. People tend to model what works. You do not have to be an innovator to make a lot of money. All you need to do is be able to determine what is selling and how you can sell it to.

You can bet your avocado balls that if you starting selling your avocado balls and it became a huge success that pretty soon businesses selling similar avocado balls will be springing up all over the place. Why? Because other people saw your success and want some of it for themselves.

While it is possible to start a new market for something, chances are that unless you have a really new of different type of product that someone has already tried selling it before. There are relatively few untapped markets these days. But that does not mean that if you have a truly great and unique product that you cannot gather a following for it.

So what you are going to have to do is look at the marketplace and determine if you think you are going to be able to crack into it. If your business is going to be an online business then you can just go ahead because the amount of money you are placing at risk is very small. But before cleaning out your 401K and mortgaging your home to start a business, you need to understand the market you are about to enter.

Here are a few things to consider when determining if your business has a legitimate chance of succeeding in an already semi-competitive marketplace:

Who is Your Competition?

Unless you have a truly unique and one of a kind product that does something nothing else has ever done, you will face some competition in your marketplace. While this is not necessarily a bad thing, you must be aware of your competition and know who your competition is, what they offer to their customers, and what you will have to offer your customers to remain competitive and even show an advantage over them.

You cannot expect to be successful if you do not have in-depth analysis of your competition. Remember that you will be the newcomer to the group and that you will have to offer something bigger or better or cheaper to lure customers away from the places where they already feel secure or comfortable.

How Well are they Known?

Are your going to have to go up against another small business or relatively unknown newcomer or are you going to have to go head to head against a well-known and respected national chain retailer?

If you have used or done business with any of your competition, how do you feel about them? Do they have a great reputation or a poor one? This is important because you are going to have to compete for the same group of customers and you will either have an advantage or disadvantage depending on how well know and what kind of reputation your competition already has in the marketplace.

What do They Offer?

Whenever you are starting a new business you are going to have to consider how you are going to enter the marketplace in order to be successful.

It usually is not good enough to create a business that is equal to your competition. In order to grab customers from where they shop now and are comfortable and somewhat secure, you are going to have to offer them something better, cheaper or unique.

Before you can create something that is better or unique, you have to know what everyone else is offering. This way you can see what the benchmark has been set on. You can look at the competition product selection and decide to offer more. You can look at their hours and improve yours to offer more accessibility. You can take their delivery service and make it better, more convenient or cheaper.

But you cannot do any of this if you do not know what the other businesses are offering. So go and visit your competition and make note of what they offer to their customers. Be specific and inquire about their various policies such as refunds and exchanges and whether they offer free delivery or delivery for a charge.

If possible talk to their customer or get an idea about what it is that people like and dislike about that business. Both likes and dislikes are important. Dislikes give you insight on what is important and what you could concentrate on. Likes let you know what people really so you can try and improve on that as well.

How is Your Product Better?

Like we have already stated, it is not good enough to offer the same as what everyone else is offering. When you enter a market for the first time you are going to have to be better or offer better because customers are already used to buying from someone else. They are likely to continue buying elsewhere unless you can give them a reason to do something different and purchase from you instead of where they are buying now.

So your products need to be better or cheaper or easier to use. They should have as many features that customers want as well. In fact, now would be a great time to go back to the previous chapter where we outlined the things that every good product needs to have. Try and hit as many of those as possible so that your products are the best options for the customers.

Do not settle for products or a business that is "good enough". This is important because most of the time good enough is not likely to really be good enough to take someone else's customer away from them and bring them over to your business.

What Can Your Business Offer that is Better?

As we said, if your business is to really succeed, it should offer something that is better than what customers can get elsewhere.

Since you are now in the stage of building your business and choosing your products, it is the perfect time to create something bigger and better for your customers.

Try to see how others are doing business and then make your business better than the others. This might be difficult because you might lack the resources that established business might have but try to find at least one important thing that you can do better than your competition. Then, take that one thing and market your business accordingly.

If there are several things you can do better than make the effort to do as many things better as possible. Different aspects of your business will be more important to some people than others so the more benefits you can offer the more likely it will be that someone finds something of real value in your business. If they find that one thing that means a lot to them then they will become a customer of yours and not your competition.

Is there Anything about Your Product or Business that is Unique or Proprietary?

We are going to talk about this in more detail in a future chapter but if there is anything special about you or your business that gives you an edge in the market, you need to identify this and understand how to apply it to your marketing and promotion.

Breaking into a new market can be tough and time consuming at times but if there is something unique or special about you or your business that can make it a lot easier for you to become successful in less time than it might normally have taken.

Know Your Costs & Expenses

In order for any business to be successful, it must actually stay in business. That means it either has to have resources available to sustain it through the early stages or tough times or it must generate enough sales and profits to cover expenses. But before we know how much we have to set aside or create in sales each month we need to know what our expenses are going to be on a monthly basis moving forward.

Profit is gross sales minus expenses so if we want to make a greater profit we either have to make more sales or reduce expenses. Expenses will come in all shapes and sizes from the cost of rent or a domain name to the cost of producing products and creating inventory. We will also have administrative costs and possibly shipping costs and packaging expenses. These are just a few of the many expenses you might incur in your business.

Understanding expenses is important because how much it costs you to stay in business and produce products will be a major determining factor when it comes to properly pricing your products. Since every product will have a certain cost to produce and ship to a customer, you need to understand these costs so you can set a fair price on that product. If you do not take the time to understand costs, you might wind up selling your products for a loss until you realize there is a problem! By then it might be too late.

When starting your business, make a list of as many of the known expenses you will have and try and be as specific and thorough as you possibly can. If you are not sure of the exact amount of a particular expense, over estimate it slightly to give yourself a little bit of a cushion. It is better to be happy when expenses turn out to be slightly lower than it would be to be surprised when expenses turn out drastically higher!

Include expenses like rent, administrative, taxes, utilities, packaging, shipping, supplies, advertising, promotion and all other expenses that might apply to your business. Do not leave anything out. It would probably be helpful to split the expenses into groups such as administrative, product costs and shipping. This would enable you to get a better handle on where you money is going every month.

As far as products are concerned, usually the more your order of an item the less it costs per unit. So it might make sense to order in larger quantities. But that also will require a larger outlay of funds in the beginning which you might not have at your disposal. In those cases you might decide to make a little bit less in profit in the very beginning and use the money that comes in from initial sales to place a bulk order at a lower price point in the future.

These are the decisions that every business owner needs to make in order to make the most profit while spending the least amount of money. It is often a balancing act where the business owner struggles with deciding where to spend what amount of money to get the most impact or benefit.

Packaging is another area where the new business owner should understanding the costs involved in getting the products to the customer. Often times the size or shape of the package can result in a widely varying shipping costs. This can mean the difference from having a competitive price or a more expensive price.

Tyr and design packaging that makes the product less costly to get into the hands of the customer. Always remember that shipping costs are not profit centers for the business and every penny paid in shipping does not benefit the customer or the business in any way.

It just benefits the shipping company. So if you can reduce shipping costs by one dollar that is easier one dollar more profit for you or one dollar less in cost for the customer. Either one helps both parties.

Understanding costs enables the business owner to get more out of their money and other resources. Understanding exact costs also allows the business to negotiate better rates and to better compare vendor costs as well. When you go into a meeting with a vendor or manufacturer armed with specific facts and figures this lets them know that they are dealing with someone who understands business and is on top of things. This will make it harder for them to take advantage of you.

Your accountant will also be able to help you take various facts and figures and enable you to make sense out of them and use them to help you grow your business. Sometimes numbers don't mean much until you place in in the right perspective and then everything becomes clear. So pay close attention, especially in the beginning as you learn about your business and the costs and expenses required.

Last, but certainly not least, knowing and monitoring your expenses also allows you to spot problems and inaccuracies earlier I the process.

These might occur if someone was stealing money from your business or otherwise manipulating the books to conceal fraudulent behavior. In these days of cyber-theft and other digitally caused financial problems, staying on top of things all the time will minimize these events from happening to you while minimizing the effect when they do.

Your Unique Market Position

Every business needs to have something difference or special about them to succeed I the marketplace. The more a business stands out from the rest of the crowd the better their overall chances of success will be. But just being different is not all that matters. It is also making sure others are aware of what is different about you so they can see why your business is better than anyone else's.

There is a term that is used to refer to why a business is different from many of the other in a certain area or market. That term is called "Unique Marketing Position" and it refers to the different things pertaining to that business that make it different from the competition. These differences might not always translate into being better or worse but they are differences none the less.

Being better is great but it will only benefit you when other people are aware of the things that make you better.

If you offer amazing benefits and prices but no one is aware of it, then those benefit, even though great for the customer, will do you little good. So not only do we have to be better, we need to make sure that everyone knows why we are better and what we have to offer.

For example, if you offer free delivery while everyone else charges for it, that could be a huge customer benefit. But if you just add free delivery without making the customer aware of it, they might not see the value in it. They might compare your price to the price elsewhere and purchase the product somewhere else because it is $10 cheaper and then pay $50 for delivery and never think twice about it.

But if you advertised free deliver and told people that delivery is free and not a $50 upcharge like it was elsewhere then customers would be made aware of that benefit and see the value in it. The likely result would have been that they would have purchased the product from you rather than elsewhere because of the benefit that you offered that they are now aware of. So merely offering something great is not enough. You need to make people aware of the value of what you offer as well.

You can arrive at your unique marketing position in one of two ways.

You can compare your business to the competition and arrive at what you offer that is different and better and then create your unique marketing position. This is that way a lot of businesses do it and while it does work, it is not the best of most efficient way of doing it.

Here's a better way:

Check out your industry or type of business against yours and see how you measure up or compare. Then compare your business to your specific competition and see how you compare against them as well. List your difference and advantages.

Then, take the areas where your business is equal to or worse than the competition and then improve those areas so that your business is better than everyone else's. The more things about your business that you can improve the stronger and more powerful your business will become.

After you have gone through all those exercises you will have created a very powerful and much more diverse unique marketing position. You will have more benefits which will make your business appeal to a much wider audience. Since different people find value in different things, the more your business can stand out the more likely it is going to be to attract new customers.

The, take your unique marketing position and make it a part of every advertisement and every sign that is in your store or on your webpages. Take every major advantage your business offers and integrate it into every aspect of your business. If you offer free delivery, then make sure every price includes a little note that says "+FREE Deliver (a $50 Value!)" so that your customers will realize the value you offer.

If you offer the largest selection, make sure your customers know about it!

If you service what you sell, let your customers know that!

If you offer free set up in the home, let your customers know!

If you have a Rewards Program or Loyalty Program, make sure your customers know!

Your unique marketing position is why your business is so special and provides such a valuable experience to your customers. You need to take advantage of every advantage you offer. You need to educate your customers on why your business is so great and so customer-focused.

Do NOT leave it for the customer to connect the dots and realize why you are so great! Be up-front and in their face about it so there is no doubt that your business is where they should be shopping. Anything less is like leaving money on the table when it comes to present and future business.

Protecting Yourself

This is the time where we need to remind you that any business, no matter what type of products you sell or which services you deliver, can be subject to lawsuits and other legal action. We live in a very lawsuit oriented culture it seems so it just makes sense to make sure you are protected when it comes to lawsuits and other claims against your business.

First and foremost you should protect yourself against legal claims by conducting your business is a very honest and above board manner. That means no misrepresenting your products, no false promises, deceptive advertising or any other behavior that could leave you open to legal action or fines and penalties.

Unfortunately, even the best efforts might still leave you open to a lawsuit and you need to protect yourself and your assets from those lawsuits. Even though we are not lawyers and are no substitute for qualified legal representation here are a few things to consider when it comes to protecting you and your business:

Get a Good Lawyer & Accountant

Nothing will protect you more from legal issues and troubles than a great accountant and lawyer. Though they will cost you money, they can both advise you in the beginning as you set up your business and then all along the way as situations require. Having both on a retainer basis is a smart way for every business owner to handle these problems.

Plus, unless you are starting just an online business you will have the need for lawyers to draw up and read contracts anyway. Search out a good lawyer for your type of business and listen to them. Don't for a minute think that you can read a contract and understand it without the help of a lawyer. Just one wrong word or wrong guess and you could be in real trouble.

Sometimes when problems do arise just a letter or response from a lawyer is enough to get people to back off. You would be surprised at how many people will threaten legal action looking for a quick score or settlement but then back off when they see you have a lawyer on your side. It is sad but still true that people behave this way.

Open the Right Type of Business

When you open your business you will have a few different options and you should discuss these with your lawyer and accountant.

There are corporations, partnerships and other forms of businesses that each have their own set of advantages and disadvantages from both legal and financial perspectives.

Corporations, for example, has the ability to shield your personal assets from business assets so if you do have a lawsuit against your business that they cannot touch your home, personal savings or possessions. This can be a real big advantage if this is the type of business you want. Again, your accountant and lawyer should advise you so you make the right decision for your own situation.

Get Insurance

Insurance will help protect you from minor lawsuits and small to medium damage claims. Depending on the cost and coverage, this might be a smart expense for you. Check with your accountant and lawyer to find out what kind and how much coverage you will need for your type of business.

Pick Safe Products

Stay away from products that have a poor history or reputation or products that are prone to high lawsuits.

For example, selling books is fairly safe is you represent them properly but if you see medical supplement or other health food supplement or vitamins that might leave you open to a lawsuit for heal reasons.

I would also stay away from products that are dangerous to use as well unless you protect yourself with a strong disclaimer and liability release. Your lawyer can prepare various releases and other documents to protect your business from claims against manufacturers that you are brought into.

Market Products & Services Honestly

A LOT of lawsuits come from exaggerated claims and false advertising. If you are marketing a product, do it honestly. Do not inflate its capabilities or performance. Do not make it appear as a wonder solution for everything. Keep claims accurate and make sure you include a disclaimer protecting yourself against manufacturer's claims which may or may not be accurate.

This will also help protect your business image by giving you a reputation for honesty and ethical marketing of all your products. You should be in business and market for the long-term relationships not the short-term gains so market honestly and always stand behind your products with refunds and other support.

Beware of Claims and Use Disclaimers

The next time you buy a product, take a quick look at the manuals that come with it and sometimes are also on the back of the receipt or contract. These disclaimers can be pages long and protect the manufacturer against just about anything. Some disclaimers are meant to intimidate people and are not worth the paper they are written on. Just because someone says they are not liable does not mean that they aren't.

Get with your lawyer to determine what kind of disclaimers and releases you should use in your business to protect yourself from lawsuit happy customers and the lawyers that they hire. While most legal claims have some validity, there will always be a certain percentage of people who will see a lawsuit as a chance to make some quick money and they always seem to find a lawyer who is more than happy to take their case.

Make Sure You Have Licenses & Releases Where Necessary

Every business has to operate within the laws and rules governing that type of business. Ignorance is not an excuse and if you violate the law or break the rules you will likely pay a hefty fine and might even lose your business.

Your local government and your accountant and lawyer will help you navigate through the maze of paperwork and also let you know what kind of requirements owning the business is likely to have. That includes getting all the proper licenses, having the right amount of insurance and paying all the taxes and fees on or before their due date.

This is only part of what might be involved in your area when it comes to opening your own business. As we have already stated we are not lawyers and we do not pretend to know everything you need to know about operating a business in your area. That is why we always strongly advise, like we are doing right now, that everyone starting their own business consult with a lawyer and accountant throughout the process.

A little bit of money spent now could save you a ton of money and aggravation later. The longer you stay in business the more likely it will be that you will have some kind of legal problem or issue. Having the right people in your corner will make those time much easier to deal with.

Start-Up Costs
& Finances

Since you are reading this book we figure that you have at least some interest in starting your own business and you did not just come up with the idea yesterday or today. If you did, that's wonderful as well but we are moving forward with the idea that you have some money to start your business with.

If you are like most people and are starting your business as a part-time business to supplement your income, that is good because you will have your regular income to help fund your business and pay your bills until your business gets some traction in the market. That can take anywhere from a few weeks or months to a year or more depending on the products and business type.

I strongly urge everyone NOT to quit their day job when they start their new business because no matter how hard we plan and how careful we are throughout the process we can never be totally sure that our business is going to be a success.

Because of this it is nice to have the security of a paycheck still coming in while we go through the start-up process.

I also understand that if you start some kind of businesses, usually the brick and mortar type that you are going to have spend a LOT of time operating your business and in those cases you are not going to be able to keep your full time job during this period of time. If that is the case and you are a married couple, consider one person keep their job while the other dedicate time to the business. The best of both worlds might even be for each of you to work a different shift in your "day job" so that between the two of you you can build the business while both of you are still working.

This is not to say that this will be easy but it is the safest way to protect your personal finances for the near future. Then, as the business starts to show signs of success you can constantly re-evaluate your work schedules and finances and determine when one, then both, of you will be able to quit and dedicated your total time and efforts to your business.

We mentioned already that over 90% of all new businesses fail and while that is not designed to scare you or deter you from starting your own business, it is designed to give you a glimpse into the reality of owning your own business. Once you come to grips with the reality of things, you will understand the importance of still having that primary income coming in every month.

As we said there are going to be expenses that you are going to have to pay before your business gets its first sale. You are going to have to buy a domain or rent a building and you are going to have to get products, procure inventory and purchase other things just to prepare yourself for doing business and creating sales.

While it should be your desire and goal to keep these initial expenses as low as possible there are limits to how low you can go and still create a viable business. While technically you could take orders and then order inventory to fulfill those orders, most of the time customers are not going to want to wait for their products so they will just go someplace where they can just pick them off the shelf and take them home. So not purchasing inventory to save money is not a good idea. So create a balance where you can provide a good level of service to the customer while keeping expenses down.

After you open the doors you should not expect orders to fly in and the business become profitable overnight. Instead there is going to be some kind of delay before your sales can fully support the business. During this time you will have to pay either all the expenses or just a portion of them until sales catches up with expenses.

This is one reason why so many people fail when starting their business. They save the money required to start the business but then do not have enough to sustain it during the initial growth period. So the business opens, money gets tight and finally when the resources dry up, the business closes and all is lost.

That is why it is so important to not only have start-up expenses covered but also up to a year of resources to pay your bills and support your business. Even that might not be enough but a year will help give you an idea of whether the business you have is going to be successful or not. As long as you see progress and the business shows signs of becoming profitable, you would want to keep it going.

Now that we hopefully agree on all of this, let's talk about where these resources and money are going to be coming from.

Some people save for a long time, use savings they already had or come into an inheritance or other kind of windfall. These people are using money they already have and that is probably the best form of financing.

But other people are not that fortunate and in fact, want to start their own business in the hopes of being able to have some extra money to set aside for the future or to improve their lifestyle. So the same people that want to earn more money and need more money the most, are the ones that probably do not have access to it. And that's where things can get dangerous and nasty very fast.

I have always said that everyone has dreams. We all have hopes and dreams about what we would like to do and have in life. While we should pursue those dreams and try to turn them into reality, we also must realize that not all dreams do come true and that other dreams have to eventually deal with reality.

When people who do not have the money to start a new business turn to second or third mortgages and personal loans to finance their business they are placing their entire future at risk. If the business should fail, which many do in the first two years, then they could lose their home, their retirement savings and still be left to pay off considerable debt.

Unfortunately people who have the most to lose often cling to the thinnest of hopes. They see or read about some person who took a dream and $100 and turned it into a multi-million dollar empire. They see success stories and think "Why can't that happen to me?" While it can happen to you it is also important to remember that for every 5 people who make it big, there can be 95 people who fail. That is just the facts when it comes to opening a business.

This does not mean you should not try. It just means that you should be careful and never invest more than you can afford to lose in any business.

If you have a great idea or a great product, be responsibly with it. Don't invest more in anything than you can safely afford to lose or at the very least, recover from.

If you are 25 and empty your retirement account to fund a great idea and it goes bad, you still have 40 years ahead of you to recover from that and save money to retire on. But if you spend it all on a great product that flops and you are 60 years old, you are too late to ever recover.

But even if you don't have a dime to your name that does not mean you have to abandon your dreams. You just have to find alternate ways to get the money and resources you need to achieve that dream. You just need to find a responsible way to fund your efforts.

People have taken part-time jobs, sold goods on the street corners or at flea markets or even done door to door sales in order to earn the money they need to finance their new business. It is up to you to determine how to go about getting the money you need to do the things you want to do. It is part of being an entrepreneur and something you must be willing to do.

You might even be willing to take on a partner or partners to help you achieve your dreams. The point is that you can achieve your dreams in a responsible way if you look and try hard enough.

But do not put your future at risk on something that will never be a sure bet. It is one thing to believe in you and your idea and another thing altogether to be irresponsible with your money.

If you have an accountant, then consult with him on how much money you should have on hand and where that money should be coming from. They will advise you on the options that are available to you and let you know why some of them make more sense than others. Plus, they have one other advantage that you don't.

They are not blinded by their own idea or their own hopes and dreams. They will see your idea or product for what it really is not what you want it to be. They will be able to determine what you actual chances of success might be and their judgment will not be clouded by your personal dreams and situations. In other words, they can give you the cold-hard facts about your business idea and how you are going to fund it.

Listen to them and never invest more than what you can afford to lose in any investment and that includes your own business.

The Shoestring Business - Open a Business for $50 or Less!

Contrary to popular belief, it does not need to cost a fortune to start a real profit generating business. IN this chapter we are going to show you how you can start your own business for less than $50. In fact, if you really work at it and do a bit of searching for the lowest cost sources, you might be able to do it for less than $25! But let's keep it easy and real and start learning how you can start your own business for $50.

On-Line Businesses

The main component of an on-line business is the domain name. This is enables people to search for your particular site among the millions of websites out there. The name you choose is important because it should describe what type of website you are creating or the type of products you sell.

For example, if you were selling handmade sweaters, a good domain name might be "handmadesweaters.com" but if you were selling all kinds of handmade clothes a better name would be "handmadeclothes.com" because it is a broader term that more accurately describes your products.

You can purchase a domain from services such as godaddy.com for less than $15.00. Sometimes they run sales when you can get a domain name for less than $10. You don't need any of the options or frills Godaddy or other domain services they offer at this point. Just get your domain name.

The next piece of the puzzle is going to be finding a hosting plan for your domain. Hosting is the service that actually places your site out on the Internet. So when people type your domain name into their browser the hosting company provides your site to the viewer. There are many kinds of hosting companies and each one has many different plans.

Do a search under domain hosting and you will find a ton of options for you to choose from. Depending on your particular needs at this point, one of the less expensive plans should be enough for you. You can always expand later should you need more disk space and bandwidth (the amount of data your site uses every month).

You should expect to pay about $5-$10 a month for hosting with a lot of the plans at or near the $5 range. Some plans bill you every month while some offer you a discount to pay for a year upfront. Choose the plan that works for you.

You should choose hosting that offers Cpanel (which most do) and has at least 25 e-mail accounts in the plan. This will give you flexibility down the road a bit. Also, you should have WordPress included in your plan as well but I have yet to see a hosting plan that did not include it.

Now that we have hosting and a domain name we have to link the servicers on our hosting plan to the domain name which is done through where you purchased your domain. They can help you set the name servers so your new domain points to your hosting company.

So far we have spent less than $25 and we technically are in business. You have a site that is live and searchable. Now all you need to do is create the content for your site and people will find it. You still have about $25 left and you can use that for a variety of items you might need to enhance your business. But you should be aware that there are also free alternatives out there that will enable you to do more for less money.

As far as content for your website there are a few options. There are free website builders out there as well as some paid software programs.

Adobe Dreamweaver is expensive but allows you to do a lot as long as you don't mind a long learning curve. Depending on your hosting company, most of them include website builders in their hosting package which means you use their templates and just copy and paste in your content. This is a very easy way to get your first site online.

If you really want an easy way to build your site you can also create a WordPress Blog which is a type of content management system that makes it easy to create nice looking websites. You can add a ton of special features and functionality by using WordPress "plug-ins" that are available either for free or for purchase that allows you to do just about anything,

If you decide to go with WordPress you can just install it for free through your hosting control panel and you are good to go! After you get used to it WordPress is easy to use. There are even a few page builders for WordPress that make it downright simple.

At this point I would suggest you try out some of the free services and tools out there for most of your needs. But if you are going to have a complex website that is going to require considerable work to set up, you might want to consider learning on one of the more professional fee-based programs that will help you do what you need to do.

The learning curve will be longer and the cost will be higher but you will just have to learn once instead of learning the free program and then moving to the more costly options later on.

Speaking of free options, there are free hosting programs out there but I caution against using them. These plans, while free, often supplement their earnings by placing ads on your pages and this can give your site a "cheap" feel and make it look unprofessional. If you do not have money for hosting you could start off on a free service but I would migrate over to a good fee-based program as soon as possible.

Another reason for this is that whenever you use a free program to do anything, you are at the mercy of the service that provides that free material. Since your business is going to hopefully make you a lot of money, you do not want to waste advertising dollars and promotion to a site that is owned by others and could disappear at a moment's notice whenever they decide to pull the plug on the free hosting service.

It is not that expensive to own your domain name and host it privately. We are talking $25 to start and $5 a month after that. This should be well within the reach of anyone who is serious about his or her new business.

So now we have a domain name and a website up and running and we might have spent under $25 accomplishing all of this. Perhaps it might be a good idea to purchase a book on how to create websites with the remaining $25. But keep in mind that there is a lot of information available for free on-line that will teach you all you need to know for free. You might have to spend some time to find it but it's out there!

Brick & Mortar (Retail Businesses)

Anyone can start a retail type business by working out of their home or other location without having to rent a building or build their own building. Often times all you will need is an idea or product and you are set to go. The only thing you need to concern yourself with is any licenses that may be required in your town or area. You can check with local government for details on appropriate licensing.

Home-based business usually work best when you are selling services such as lawn maintenance, pool cleaning, house cleaning or similar types of services. You advertise a phone number and people call you and you give them a price and schedule the service. This works very well while also allowing you to start your business very economically.

In fact, many large and successful business maintained their home based status long after they became successful because it still worked so well for them.

Selling products might be more difficult because you would either have to deliver every product or have people come to your home to pick them up and that is not a really good situation to put yourself in. But if what you are selling is able to be shipped, the home-based model could work for you as well.

You have to get a license and then have some form of advertising such as an ad in a local paper or flyers that you walk around and place in people's mailboxes. This is where creative thinking and ingenuity come into play. When you read about what some multi-millionaires did to start their business you would see how unconventional methods resulted in some pretty impressive businesses.

The point is that you can do this if you are willing to do certain things and put in certain efforts. You need to decide if you are going to let an obstacle stop you dead in your tracks or if you are going to be one of those people who find a way to work around obstacles to get what they want in life. It is your decision and your future is going to be written upon what you decide and do today.

The important thing to remember is that money does not need to be an obstacle that prevents you from following your dreams.

In the next chapter we are going to discuss ways of getting your business started and keep it going using low or no cost options that are available to almost everyone. They might not be glamourous or exciting but they do work. So if you really want to get your own business off the ground but have no money, we will show you how to do that as well.

Low & No-Cost Options

No matter what type of business you run, it is not reasonable to expect yourself to know how to do every single task that is required to set up a good looking and highly functioning business. While you will be able to do a lot of things, you cannot expect yourself to be a master of everything.

Plus, being able to purchase services or software or hire out various tasks or project might be too expensive for you as well. Usually we do have limits on what we can afford when we are just starting our business.

Because of both of these factors, there will be times when we are going to need help in getting things done in a cost effective and timely manner. Fortunately there are several ways to get things done at little or no out of pocket cost. In this chapter we are going to look at some of the options we might be able to utilize in helping start or grow our business.

Brick & Mortar Businesses

Government Small Business Programs

The government has a lot of programs designed to help people build successful small businesses. These programs will help you get the information and expertise you need to get your business started in the right way.

There are also programs to help with financing your new business as well. Here you might find low cost loans or grants that will help you get the things you need to start your business without paying the high interest of standard credit.

Small Business Incubators

If you have one of these in your area they can be a huge help. They offer low cost office space with telephone and secretarial support as well as many other services that would be too costly for you to get for just yourself. You would have access to these services and space for a certain period of time as you build your business. Then, when the business is established, you would transfer over to your own private space and operate your business on your own.

These incubators are not only cost effective but they also put you in contact with other people who are also building their own businesses and you can learn from each other and help each other as needed. You can build very worthwhile contacts in this manner which will help you now and later as your business grows,

Mentorship Programs

There are also programs where business owners mentor new business owners and show them how to best start and grow their own business. This kind of expertise can be invaluable for the new business owner. That is because experience is almost always the best teach and whenever you can learn from someone who has actually done what you are trying to do they can save you time, money and resources by letting you learn from their mistakes.

Local Trade or Business Organizations

If your business has a trade association or local association consider reaching out and joining the organization. Not only will you find out more about your business and how to grow it you will also find out more about the industry and how your business could play a bigger role in it.

One mistake business owners usually make when it comes to trade associations and other member-based organization is that they try to use that organization as a group to try and sell to and that is not a good idea. People will come to you and your business when they need it and only if you behave properly during meetings. These associations do not exist for members to sell to one another. They exist for the mutual benefit of the members.

Partners

One option that is always open when you lack a particular skill or activity and cannot out-source or learn it is to take on a partner that already possesses that particular skill or knowledge. This does not cost you anything out of pocket but will cost you equity in the business. But if you need financing or specific knowledge this could be the best way to start your business off and get it functioning at a high level almost immediately.

We might even be able to enter a partnership with another company to handle certain parts of your business for you. An example might be partnering up with a shipping company to handle all your shipping and delivery tasks for you.

You pay them a fee and they handle everything for you sparing you the headaches of setting everything up, hiring employees and taking care of the day to day issues.

Outsourcing

There are people and business available for hire that can provide any skill or knowledge you may ever need. You just hire them for a specific job or task, they do it and you pay them. There is no loss of equity, no salary to pay and you pay them only when you need them.

This could be the short-term answer to your short-term needs but there are two important things to remember when comparing an outsourcer to an employee or partner. Out-sourcers get paid by the job and will have little or no loyalty or incentive to do a great job for you. So you might not get the highest quality work or have the attention to detail that you might get from an employee or partner that has a vested interest in the company.

Second, and this could be very important, whenever you out-source something you might have to provide specific information that may be confidential or restricted. Whenever you share this outside the company you do run the risk of someone taking that knowledge and using it to hurt your business, steal your products or take away your customers.

Even though this type of activity is unethical, it has been known to happen. Some people have no boundaries when it comes to making money.

Bartering

Sometimes if you have a particular skill that someone wants and they have something you want you can arrange a trade where you take care of something for them and they take care of something for you. Or you provide products in exchange for services or vice versa. If you both have something the other one needs this could work out well for you. But it is more difficult to find someone who has what you need and at the same times needs something you have.

On-Line Businesses

Free Software

Fortunately, or unfortunately as the case may be, online businesses usually revolve around some kind of software either for website creation or product creation. Some of this software is very expensive. Photoshop, for example costs several hundred dollars and this might be out of your reach at the beginning of your business.

The same applies to webpage building software such as Abode Dreamweaver which also goes for hundreds of dollars.

There are some free alternative to some popular software and those should be checked out before you make any commitment to expensive software. For example there is an equivalent to Photoshop called GIMP that is free. There is a great audio sound mixing program called Audacity that will put a studio recording console on you PC and that is free as well.

As far as word processing is concerned there is a substitute for Microsoft Office call Open Office that is free to users. Add to this list free copies of website builders, free WordPress plug-ins and other software and you can do just about everything and pay nothing. You might sacrifice a few bells and whistles but it will usually be enough to get you started!

Free Information

One thing the internet is great for and that is providing free information on just about any topic you can imagine. When it comes to building a business, this is certainly not the exception. No matter what aspect of business building you might need help with, you will find almost unlimited articles, blog posts, advice or even full courses on. All you have to do is search for what you need.

This works well also for brick and mortar businesses as well. Whenever you need any kind of information or need guidance on how to set up and auto-responder to create a basic webpage, there is wealth of information for you and most of it is free. Of course there are also e-books and fee-based courses as well but even those are usually much cheaper than seminars held at your local university or hotel.

One quick observation and warning though: Just because you read something on-line does not mean it is 100% accurate. So check what you are reading to make sure it is accurate. Also, finding information is getting harder and harder these days because everyone is using articles and reviews as thinly disguised sales pitches for whatever products that person is selling. So what you are reading is not intended to educate but instead to get you to purchase a particular product! So reader beware!

Low-Cost Outsource Sites

Some people love these sites where people can post a task and have someone agree to do it for just a few dollars. The most well-known site is called FIVERR.com and you can post any legal task you want done and people will go it for $5.

You might need a picture edited or a logo designed or an article written. No matter what it is people will do it cheaply. Most of the time cheaper than you would be able to do it yourself. But there are concerns as well that the buyer should be aware of.

First, you are responsible for the content on your website. So if you pay someone to write an article for you and they just steal something already written and you post it on your website, you could be sued for copyright violation. If you ask for a picture of something and someone sends you a picture they copied from another publication, you could get sued for copyright there as well.

As usual what started out as a great way to get some things done for a small free has now been monetized and twisted so that people try to get the most money by providing the least in effort and people get hurt. Just remember that ignorance is not an excuse and if you use something that was stolen by someone else on your website, you are liable.

In my opinion these type of sites are good for the occasional or "one-off" type of jobs that come up once in a while. But for jobs that you will need done on a fairly consistent basis, you are much better off trying to find one person that you can go back to time and time again for that type of work. Knowing that they are likely to continue receiving additional work from you in the future as long as they continue to do a good job will motivate them to give their best efforts to your work.

Free Services

While there are many free services out there to handle a number of tasks and functions for your business, they often come at a steep price. Free hosting, for example, might seem like a real good deal except when you take a look at your site and see little ads that you did not place on the site but were placed by the hosting company. Revenue from these ads is how they make their money.

But all of those "extra ads" may or may not blend in nicely with the rest of your site and tend to give it a "cheap" fell or look that takes away from your content. Not only that but every time someone clicks on one of those ads they are taken away from your site and you might wind up losing sales as a result.

The same goes for those free e-mail sites like Gmail and Yahoo. Those e-mail addresses just about shout out "cheap" or "garage-based business" to your visitors. Almost every hosting company includes the ability to set up e-mail accounts for free on your domain services. The result is a professional looking and sounding e-mail address instead of one of the cheesy ones. Those have their place with private individuals but not with businesses.

Another thing with free e-mails is that they often have their own "messages" at the bottom from the e-mail company and these have no place on e-mails to or from your business. When it comes to e-mails and your business, stick to e-mail addresses from your own domain accounts for the best look and impression.

There are free auto responders available as well and these are good to get you started. Just make sure that you are able to export your mailing list at any time so that should you want to move to another company or privately host your own auto responder that you will be able to take your list with you. But there are a couple of companies that will allow you to build a list of up to 2,500 people for free so this should be enough to get you started.

By all means check out free alternatives but make sure they do not taint your brand by adding advertisements or messages and always personally view their effect on your webpages and e-mails. Remember you will take a long time to build your brand and reputation but it only takes a short time to ruin it.

Automation

One of the best things about an online business is that you can automate so much of the sales process.

If you are in the business of selling information products, for example, you can automate the entire process so that orders are automatically processed and sent to buyers within minutes of them completing the payment process.

Not only does this make running your business and easier and keeps you from having to manually process orders, it also helps the customer because they get what they bought almost immediately and everyone loves getting stuff quickly. Automation also allows you to have orders filled and for you to make money even when you are away or on vacation.

Automation is usually done by a digital delivery system of which there are many. While you can set this up manually with auto responders and such doing it manually does make it much easier for people to steal your products and even sell them to others and have you ship them to their customer while they take all the profit!

There are many digital delivery systems out there and they range from under $100 to several hundred dollars. I have found that the cheaper ones will do just fine for most businesses. In fact the one that I use has been discontinued for over 10 year and has been replaced by a program with a lot more features.

But the old one serves me just fine so I keep using it. Search under digital delivery systems and find one that appeals to you. There will be a learning curve associated with setting up each of your products but most of these are easy to use once you get used to them.

Another automated system you should use is an auto responder. Auto responders are programs that will automatically send out a series of e-mails to the people on your list at predetermined times. This allows you to offer digital courses or a series of e-mails outlining particular information or knowledge to your members. You can also use these for automatic marketing as well.

You can purchase auto responder programs and self-host them or go with one of the common third party systems such as AWEBER or GETRESPONSE. These are fee-based programs that host your auto responder on their services and you set things up with their system instead of your own. They charge a monthly fee around $25 or so depending on the size of your mailing list.

Payment Services

If you want to sell products on line you will have to make it possible for people to pay for them. In the "old days" payment was made by check or via credit card.

Today, many new businesses create an on-line account with PayPal.com which enables you to accept credit cards without having a merchant account. PayPal will take a fee out of every transaction and send the rest of the money to your account.

You can link a credit card or bank account to your PayPal account so that you can transfer money in to fund purchases or out to your bank account when you want to withdraw funds from your account. You can have multiple PayPal accounts and your account name is your e-mail address and a custom password.

PayPal is by far the most popular on-line payment company and they make issuing refunds and accepting payments extremely easy for both the customer and the business. Customers can use their regular credit card to purchase and business can issue refunds directly through PayPal. It is so easy your sales are likely to increase when you allow people to purchase with PayPal.

There is no fee to open an account. They will deduct a small fee from every sale and that is how they get paid. But since you have to pay a fee to accept credit card orders through a merchant account, the fees are not that big of a deal.

On-Line Courses

Last but not least there are a ton of websites out there that have articles, courses and books on just about any subject you can think of. No matter what your need might be, you can find it on-line and it is easier than going to the library or the local bookstore. It is cheaper as well. Search for whatever you need when you need it and you will find a lot of information when it comes to starting and running your own business.

Get Help

If I were to give you just one piece of important advice when it comes to starting your own business it would be to never try and do everything yourself. There is no shame in asking for help and you should not think of it as a weakness either. In fact, asking for help is probably one of the smartest and courageous things you can do in life. Don't let pride get in the way of you achieving the best results.

The smart business owner knows what he or she is really good at as well as the things they are poor or really bad at as well. They understand that the success of their business is going to depend on the results they will get on various tasks related to their business. If something is not done well then it might stand in the way of closing a sale or getting a customer interested in your business.

Some business owners let pride get in the way of making the right decisions. They see their inability to do something well as a personal insult or failure. Since they do not like sharing their supposed failures with others, they do the best they can even though the result is not going to be anywhere like it could have been. So they accept a mediocre effort bot because there are no other alternatives but simply because they refuse to ask for help.

Imagine how sales would be impacted by a flyer that looked "OK" instead of great!

Imagine how a poorly designed logo instead of a professionally created one might make the business look "cheap".

Imagine how a customer might be hesitant to buy from a website that looked like it was designed by someone in Kindergarten?

These are just a few of the problems that all business owners have when it comes to mastering all the different skills, talents and abilities that running your own business requires. But even though all of these skills are necessary, it doesn't mean the business owner has to have all of them in order to be successful. It doesn't even mean the business owner should have all of the skills and knowledge to do all of these things.

In fact, I do not know of anyone, business owner or otherwise, that is good at everything and is the best choice for doing every single thing in running a business.

There is always someone better to do certain things and the smart business owner realizes this and takes advantage of it. The smart business owner understands their strengths and weaknesses and gets help when it's needed.

Smart business owners learn how to delegate. By that I mean that they learn when they should do something themselves and when it makes sense to farm it out or assign it to someone else to do. There are several factors that come into play when deciding whether or not to do something yourself. Here are a few factors to consider where you might find it better to have someone else take care of something in your business:

Time

Do you have the time to do something or are you just backed up against the wall trying to meet deadlines? Sometimes we have so much to do and so little time to do it all in that we rush through things and the result is that we do not give our best effort to anything. So the results are poor all the way around.

We should give ourselves time to do things right. Whenever we find ourselves short on time it might be the smartest thing to let someone else take care of something so we can concentrate on other things that we are better at.

The other side of the time issue is that often time people who are more skilled at something can turn out a better result in much less time than we can. For example I might like to create a great looking webpage but if it takes me 3 days but someone else could do it in 2 hours, then that might be a huge waste of time and the results would probably be worse if I did it anyway. Highly skilled people can just turn out better quality work in less time than you or I can.

Skills

As frustrating as it might be, sometimes there are just people who are more skilled at doing things than we are. For example I am somewhat skilled at Photoshop but it will likely take me 3 or 4 times longer to get a less spectacular result than it would be to use someone who uses Photoshop every day.

I have people who ask me to write something for them because I can do it easier and faster than they can in less time because that is where my skill set is. It doesn't mean that I am a better person than anyone else, it just means I have a set of skills that enable me to do something a little better.

Smart business owners have several people that they rely on each with their own special set of skills. We might have someone who is great at image editing and web design and someone else who is great at creating compelling sales copy.

Plus, the have a very personable person handling direct customer contact and to resolve problems with customers because that person just does it better.

Final Results

When someone tries to go it alone and do everything, the results usually show it. In the beginning we sometimes have no other options when we have few or no contacts and money is tight as well. But as our business grows and our contact lists grow as well, we need to concentrate more on the final results when deciding who is going to do what.

Sometimes it is hard to see why something else is better. You can't put your finger on it but one image looks better than another or one piece of writing flows a bit better. One webpage looks dynamite but something else has something lacking. You can't place your finger on it but there's something missing.

So much of sales and marketing rests on the little things. The perfect word in a sales copy or the perfect image or description is what often sells a product. A successful business uses all of these little things to produce the best and most compelling urge to buy in the minds of the customers are the businesses that sell the most product and make the most money.

Think about this for a minute: Everyone who is in business is looking for any way to make their business more successful. That means creating the best store or website, carrying the best products, representing those products in the best manner and creating a business atmosphere that makes the customer want to buy from them.

These efforts are all being done to the very best of everyone's ability. Are you going to give these same things your best effort or are you going to give them the best of everyone's effort? Are you going to settle for what you are capable of doing or are you going to search out people and services that can do things better to give your business the edge it needs to succeed in a very competitive marketplace?

Importance

In business as in life, not everything carries the same level of importance. There are some things that are absolutely critical to your business, some things that are fairly important and other things that carry little importance at all. Because of this, it makes sense to make sure the critical, or very important things, get the best attention by the people best suited for those tasks.

For example, if you own a retail store, it is much more important to make the selling floor as attractive as possible so you might want enlist the help of someone skilled in creating that kind of environment.

They can set up customer flow, choose the right color scheme and product placement and take care of all the other things that go into creating the perfect customer buying experience. That can of experience is what sets successful businesses apart from others.

But what color you paint the restroom isn't all that important so you might want to tackle that room and the back offices that nobody sees. After all, the impact on choosing wrong in those areas will be very small.

Whenever you come across a task, or list of tasks, ask yourself just how important each of those tasks are. Then ask yourself if you really are the right person for doing each of those tasks. Can you do a great job or will the results just be OK? Often times that will make your decision for you. But take special care to make sure the really important things are done by the best people for that job. That might be you or it might be someone else. It doesn't matter who it is only that the right person does it and gets the best results.

Money

Sometimes it all comes down to money. You might want someone else to do something because they can do a better job but you don't have the money to pay them.

That's fine and we understand that some business owners are routinely in that position especially early in their business. Sometimes we have to do almost everything ourselves because we have to. If that's the case do the best you can until you find yourself capable of paying others to get better results as your business grows.

But sometimes it just makes no sense for you to do something because it is a poor use of your time. A good rule of thumb is that if you can make more money do something else in the same period of time then you should do that and pay someone to do less skilled tasks.

For example, if you are an excellent copywriter and can turn out fantastic sales copy in an hour, then it makes little sense for you to spend that hour doing something that is unskilled or less skilled. If you can turn out a sales letter worth $500 in an hour then you should do that instead of packing and shipping out orders. You can hire someone to do that for you.

This means you need to assign a value to your skills and to your time and then make decisions based on that. Sure, in the early days of our business we are going to write our sales copy and pack our own orders and carry them to the post office. We are going to be a one or two man show. That is fine but as our business grows we need to take stock of our own skills and use our time wisely.

Owning a business needs to be done on a result driven basis. IN other words, we need to do what gives us the greatest amount of results in the same period of time. We need to work to our strengths and find others who will add to our efforts in order to make our business grow. This might mean paying someone early on and learning from them as they work so that we can turn a weakness into a strength. But it also means understanding our weaknesses so we do not make our weaknesses our business' weaknesses.

If you need help, ask for it. If you have to pay someone to do something better and you can afford to do it, then do it. In other words, do what it takes to make your business the best and strongest business possible.

How to Market Your Products or Services Properly

Some business owner's think that all you need are good products and that once you have them, you can sit back, watch the money roll in and start planning your early retirement. Well, I hate to burst your bubble but having good products is just the first step towards building a successful business.

That is not to say that having good products and services are not important. In fact, you MUST have good quality products and high quality services in order to create and sustain a profitable and successful business. After all, people might buy from you once but if you sell or offer crap to your customers no one is going to come back a second time!

But as we said, having good products and services is just the first step. The second, and almost equally important is your ability to connect the customer to the correct product or service for his or her needs. Some people think that the customer should be the one doing that and if you think that is the correct approach you are dead wrong.

The fact is, many, if not most, of your customer will "think" they know what's the best choice for them but they might be totally wrong in their assessment. So unless you can steer them in the right direction and to the correct product choices, your business is not likely to become a huge success.

For example, if a customer thinks the lowest price product will suit their needs and it doesn't, then they will likely be mad at you and your business instead of themselves. If they purchase a product and it doesn't do what they thought it would or should do, they will be mad at the product and your business not themselves. The list could go on and on but I think you get my drift here.

It is up to you to connect the right product to the right customer.

This is where our marketing and sales assistance comes into play. Most of the time our business plan might determine our marketing strategy. If we are using a business model that stresses the lowest price or a "bargain atmosphere" then people are going to buy from you based on price and not their sales experience although that will still matter.

But if your business model is based on products and service and quality, then you need to market your products accurately and honestly.

Failure to do both will wind up costing you sales and business in the long run. It is a much better idea to represent your products for what they can do and not what you think people need them to do. Sometimes these are two very different things indeed.

Selling VS. Assisting

I have held a lot of positions over the years for several different companies and I have been successful in those positions because although I was involved in sales, I never tried to sell something to a customer.

For me, trying to sell something to someone always stood for trying to convince someone to buy something when they weren't totally sure that the product or service really fit their needs or not. I had watched other salesmen push what was on sale or what had the greatest commission or margin and that always rubbed me the wrong way.

I always looked at my job as trying to assist the customer in finding the absolute best product for his or her needs. Most of the time that resulted in a sale but there were times when the customer walked out without buying because we didn't have exactly what they needed. Some people would think that was a failure on my part but that was a shot-sighted view.

I always had people come back and ask for me because of how I treated them or "assisted" them last time they were in. the appreciated the lack of a high pressure sales pitch and they also appreciated that I only wanted to sell them what was right for them. So in the long run I closed more sales and sold more products than most other people.

When you start your business, you need to understand what your approach is going to be with your customers. Are you going to start a business with the hope of becoming known as the expert in your field or the best place to go to buy certain products? If so, then you need to market your products with that particular approach in mind.

That means marketing your products for specific application and give customers specific knowledge and insight into what they are buying. It means being feature specific and showcasing different models for what they can do that other models can't. It also means nicely explaining why certain models would not be a good fit even if that results in losing a sale.

Some businesses tell their salesmen to push products and to make sure to let customers know that those products can do anything the customer needs them to do even if the product can't do it.

The feeling is that once the product is sold and leaves the store, it is the customers problem not theirs.

The problem with that approach is that you will have more refunds, more angry customers and fewer returning customers who are likely to go elsewhere next time. Being dis-honest to lose a sale now will place your business in danger tomorrow. Don't take that route. Instead, be open and honest and assist customers in finding the best products for their needs instead of selling them something.

Know Your Products

In a lot of stores, especially those "big box" type of stores, knowledge of the actual products appears to be at an all-time low. It seems that even the simplest answers stump the salesperson who often is just filling in from another department and doesn't know the difference between a hammer and a chaise lounge. This does not speak well for the business and unless your business is based on the "low price" business model this kind of knowledge gap will hurt you.

As you start your business, get to know your products. Understanding what they do and how they do it will help you take that knowledge and use it to assist your customers. You need to have the knowledge of the product so you can take the customer's need and match it to the right product and model.

You need to know what each product can or cannot do so you can choose the best options so the customer's needs will be met but not grossly exceeded.

This is the knowledge you cannot expect the customer has but that you will need so you can best help the customer. It is also the knowledge you will use to help establish your business as the best resource for information, knowledge and assistance for all your customers. This is how a business goes from a small start-up to the go to business in the area.

Think about the times you went into a store and asked a simple question and receive an "I don't know" or "We sell them online and you can get the details on our website." Or some other unhelpful response. My personal favorite in the big box stores is "I don't usually work in this department but Tom, the guy who does, is on vacation this week," How did that response make you feel towards that business? Did it inspire faith or confidence in their ability to give you the best product for your needs? Or did it make you feel that you should probably go elsewhere, and possibly even pay more, to get the advice and assistance you need?

That should give you the answer you are looking for right there. Be knowledgeable about the products you sell and also the products your competition sells.

Then you will really be in a great position to help your customers get exactly what they need.

Know Your Customers

Just like there are several different products to address a single need there are many different types of customers as well and you need to understand and be ready for each one when they walk through the doors.

There is no one perfect sales pitch or approach to dealing with every kind of customer. Everyone will have different needs and different personalities and each one will find different things that are more important to them than they would to other customers. It is your job to identify the real need for every customer.

That means understanding your customers in your area. In the case of online businesses, it means understanding where people are coming from when they come to your site and what most people searching for your products need.

In many cases online customers are more difficult because you cannot ask your customers questions. So if you have an online business you must make a good effort to include as much information and guidance as possible in your website.

You need to make sure the questions they have when coming to your site are answered in the site and that you have as much helpful and informative content to help them make a pretty accurate decision on what products best suit their needs.

When you have a brick and mortar retail location this means taking time to understand the demographic of the people who live in your area and what their needs are likely to be. Once you understand their needs you can create the best product offering to help address those needs. This means carrying the biggest selection of the most popular products for your customers. This will vary from area to area and the smart business owner realizes that having more of what the customers want translates into more sales.

Understanding your customers also help you determine which value added services are going to be the most popular and give your business the biggest advantage over your competition. If your area is largely senior citizens, for example, free delivery and set-up might be very popular. If you are in a congested area then plenty of parking would be an asset as well. Knowing your customers and your area will help you create the most responsive and desirable business for your customers.

Solve a Problem

This is perhaps the single most important part of sales and marketing. Every single product that is for sale in any store is there because it either fulfills a need or solves a problem. If your product does not do either of these for a customer they will be hard pressed to purchase it. After all, if it doesn't fulfill a need or solve a problem, there is no reason for someone to purchase it. Do you buy things you have no need for or reason for buying? No, and your customer's wont either.

But having products that fulfill needs to solve problems is not enough. It is your job to help the customer understand the problems a product solves and the needs it addresses. You cannot assume the customer knows this because they might never have thought about it. You need to help "connect the dots" between the product and what it helps do for the customer.

For example, a customer might not be aware that the next model up helps complete a task in half the time or in half the number of steps. This might be a huge benefit to the customer that they might be totally unaware of. By making them aware of the benefits you might sell the upgraded model and not only give the customer exactly what they needed you made a larger sale as well. Remember, it is not about selling, it is about matching the customer with the best product for them.

So if there are a number or problems or needs that a product addresses, make sure customers are aware of it. Make it part of your product description or list the problems that are solved on a bullet chart on the product or advertisement. Make sure the customer is aware of everything the product can do. Keep the claims factual and honest but make sure that every benefit is shown or talked about.

It has always been said that we don't sell products but instead that we sell features and benefits. This means that we take the needs of the customer and then choose a product that addresses those needs or solves those problems. When we can convince a customer that a product does everything they need and more, we can usually close the sale very easily. Then we will have a happy customer and a business that has closed more sales.

Make Them Easy to Find

Regardless of what type of business you operate, one thing always remains extremely important. If you want more people to purchase your products, you must make them easy to find. That means creating a logical and intuitive store layout or website. If it is difficult for your customers to find what they need, they will soon just go somewhere else.

If there are two things that almost all customers dislike it spending more time than necessary or making something more difficult than it needs to be. Customers like fast and simple over slow and cumbersome and they will take it every time.

If you look at some of the biggest and most successful businesses, you will see that their business model is one of simplicity and easy of doing business. Sites like Amazon, for example, offer one click shopping where all you have to do is click one box on the website and the product is shipped to you using information on file and charged to your credit card that is also on file. No forms to fill out or pages to click through to complete you purchase.

Locations of products should be clearly labelled and like products and their accessories should be grouped together as well. This will not only make it easier for customers to find things but will also result in more add-on or spur of the moment purchases as well.

The entire focus should be on making the product selection and purchase process as fast and easy as possible. This will make your business more appealing to people and they will choose your business over others because it requires less time and effort to shop there. Of course, all of this assumes you have the quality and selection as well for the customer. If you combine quality products with ease of shopping, you will have a winner!

Price

Contrary to popular belief, prices is not the most important factor people use when deciding where to go to make their purchases. Granted price is a prime factor for business models stressing lower priced products, but generally speaking, the more expensive the product the less important price becomes in determining where to complete the purchase.

This does not mean that you do not have to make your prices competitive. It just means that price is not the only thing people consider when deciding where to purchase. Other factors such as reputation, selection, knowledge and sales help all play a significant role in the decision making process.

Price is just one aspect of the total customer experience. Such there are other parts to the customer experience that hold a certain value in the mind of the customer, we must not concentrate totally on price when building our business. In some cases, people are willing to pay a premium price to get the assistance and assurance and peace of mind that often come from purchasing from the right dealer or business.

So how should you set prices? After all, everyone would like to get the highest possible price for everything they sell and become millionaires overnight.

But that rarely happens unless you have a great product that is available only from you. If you are like most every other business, you will have to compete for sales among the other competing businesses in your area or online.

Instead, you are going to have to understand your market and geographical area and create a price point that, in conjunction with the other parts of your business, helps create a desirable reaction or opinion in the eyes of the customer.

Usually in the beginning of a new business low prices are used to get people to come through the doors. In these cases the business has less to offer in terms of security and reputation and lower prices can overcome a bit of the skepticism in the mind of customers. Then, as the business becomes better known and more respected, higher prices can be charged without damaging sales. But in the beginning, lower prices is an effective way to get people to at least come in or stop by.

But prices can only be so low before the business does not make a profit so there usually will be a limit to what you can charge and still create a healthy business. To help create a better value in the mind of the customer we can also rely on "value added extras" that might not cost you very much but have significant value in the eyes of the customer.

For example you might offer an extra year on the warranty of products you sell. Or you could have a liberal refund/exchange policy to create more reassurance in the eyes of the customer. There are many things you can do to create a higher perceived value that helps justify a higher price point.

But like we have said already, none of these value added extras or customer benefits are worth anything to your business if the customer is not aware of the value behind them. So if you offer anything better or different than your competition do not hope your customers realize it. TELL THEM and make sure they know it!

When Will I Turn a Profit?

This is the question most, if not all, new business owners ask themselves in the months or days leading up to starting their new business. They want to know when all the work and preparation is going to pay off in the form of healthy profits flowing into their bank accounts. It is a fair question that unfortunately has no easy or accurate answer.

When you are going to turn a profit is going to depend on several things all of which are going to be different for every new business. How much it cost you to start the business, what your monthly and yearly expenses are going to be, the profit margins you have on each product you sell and the amount of sales you actually make in your first few weeks or months will all have an impact on when you make a profit.

While your accountant will probably be able to give you a much better and more accurate picture based on your own situation, here are a few things you can do to help turn a profit in a shorter period of time:

Have Adequate Start-Up Capital

Most businesses fail because the new owner does not have sufficient start-up capital to sustain the business during the first year. They might have enough to open the store and stock it with products but then there is nothing left. Always plan on having at least a year's worth of funds to sustain the business and your personal life as the business starts to grow and become established.

Keep in mind that in the beginning more money has to go back into the business to create promotion and advertising to get the business better known in the community. After a while this will happen on its own but in the beginning, you are going to have to spend more than usual on marketing and promotion. All of this requires money. If you don't have it and cannot afford these expenses, the business will either grow more slowly or fail altogether.

Limit Expenses

While we need to have a certain level of expenses to sustain the business and provide great products and services to the customer we should make efforts to limit expenses as much as possible during the first year or so.

We should not limit expenses on things that impact the customer or how the business is perceived by the public but there are other areas where you can cut back especially in the beginning.

For example, maybe you take home uniform and awash them at home instead of paying a service to do it for you. Although this is more work for you it costs you much less and this can help you through the early days when profits are low. Or maybe put off the cappuccino machine purchase for the office for a while. Even $100 can mean a lot in the early days.

Whenever you are thinking about spending money on anything ask yourself if spending this money is going to impact the customer or the public. If the answer is no, then reconsider that expense. But do not cut back on expenses that enhance your business or make things better for the customer. Remember that the customer wants what they want and if you don't give it to them they will go somewhere that will.

Watch Inventory

While we are going to need enough inventory to make reasonably sure we will have products to sell when our customers need them, we should not have so much inventory that we are spending too much money, that we might not have, on excessive inventory.

Maintaining a good inventory level is a balancing act. We want to have enough so that we do not run out but not so much that we have unsolved product filling up the shelves and our back room or warehouse that will go unsold for months. Depending on our industry or type of products we sell, there may be a shelf life to the products as well.

We need to start with a reasonable inventory level and then track it closely to find out how much we sell in an average week or month and then stock accordingly. We should allow ourselves a slight overlap as far as stocking levels to account for delivery delays or backorders. For example, if we sell 50 of a product a week and it takes 2 weeks to get the product into the store from the date of ordering, then we might want to stock 3 weeks worth of product to give ourselves a one week buffer.

While it is all right to run out occasionally of some products, you do not want to get the reputation or frequently being out of something your customers need. If this is found to be the case customers will eventually become frustrated with your business and start going elsewhere. So make a good effort to manage inventory effectively and accurately and never have more than you reasonably expect to sell.

Inventory costs us money and we don't recoup that money until that inventory is sold. So while that money is not wasted, we don't want to wait two years to have that money paid back either. While sometimes it might pay to buy in larger quantities because we get lower prices per unit, we have to balance that out with the cost of carrying that inventory on the shelves for longer period of time.

I would consult with your accountant for more guidance on how you should manage your business assets as far as inventory is concerned.

Invest in Advertising and Promotion

This is one area where many new businesses make a very common mistake. In their attempts to spend less and reduce expenses they cut back on promotion and advertising. This can be deadly to a new business because unless you are in a very visible or prominent location with lots of foot traffic, advertising is the only way people are ever going to be aware that you exist.

Advertising is what is going to bring new people who had never walked through the doors before into our business. It might be the advertising of a new product or a special sale price designed to get people in to get a special deal.

In the beginning we cannot count on much word of mouth advertising because there are no people who have actually used our business before. So advertising becomes even more critical and important in the early stages as it will later. As time goes on you might find yourself needing to spend less money on advertising as your business becomes more well-known but in the beginning, cutting back on advertising is one sure way to limit your growth or even cause your new business to fail completely.

We need new customers a lot more in the beginning and advertising and promotion is what delivers them to us. Always remember that when you are thinking about saving money and do not cut advertising or promotion.

Become Known in Your Community

One of the best ways for a new business to get a head start is to become known in the community. Take part in special events, sponsor a fund raiser or other event to get your name out in front of prospective customers. Join civic organizations and help out in the community. Anything you can do to get your business name in front of people will help you get recognized.

Do NOT join organizations and use those meetings to sell stuff however as that will immediately turn everyone off and will not only not accomplish anything positive it could do your business harm. Be productive inside the organization and do things designed to help the community and get your name out there for folks to see.

This usually works out well because people tend to do business with local businesses and those who are seen to be a positive part of the community. So donate to organizations and get your ad in their program or any other printed matter that people see. Offer discounts to organizations so their members will want to come in your store.

Community involvement helps you get exposure and recognition and helps you build a community friendly brand that will bring people through your doors. Think of it as just another way to advertise and promote your business while helping out organization that do good things for others.

Put in More Time

While most of us open our own business for the freedom and wealth aspects of it, the harsh reality is that most business owners spend a lot more time working in their own business than they used to in their 9-5 jobs. But hopefully they love their new business and the extra time will not be seen as a job but rather as an investment.

Look at spending extra time this way:

If you work an extra 20 hours a week that means you do not have to hire and pay someone to work those 20 yours for you. If you pay them $10 an hour that means you have save $200 plus taxes and benefits and all the other expenses that go with hiring employees. Plus, when you work those 20 hours that means that there will be someone working in your business that will treat your customers exactly like you wanted and will work harder to make your business a success.

It is quite easy to save a thousand dollars a month by working longer hours. If you are married you can have your spouse work as well if that is appropriate. If you have other relatives or older children, get them to help out as well. Even if you pay the children and put money in the college fund, it still helps you out financially.

The idea is to cut down as much as you can when it comes to labor costs. Labor is something that you pay out and have little to show for at the end of the month unless that labor was paid to create products or build the store or accomplish something of a physical nature than benefits the business.

But instead of paying someone to clean the toiler or sweep up at the end of the day, consider doing that yourself to save a few dollars.

It might not be glamourous and it might not be something you want to do at the end of a log day, but it will help you save money. Money that might be spent on more important things or reinvested into your business. Then, when the business grows a bit, hire someone to do those things for you. You will be able to afford it then!

NOTE: There is a limit to what one person can do and how long one person can work. If you spend too many hours working in your business then you might start neglecting the people in your life and other parts of your life. You should always maintain somewhat of a balance so that you pay equal attention to everything that is important in your life.

Working too long or too hard is not good for your health either. You need to get enough sleep for your body to heel and prepare itself for the next day. You need some downtime and relaxation time as well in order to keep your immune system working well too. Plus, you should not work all day and grab fast food because you are so busy. Spend time to create and eat healthy meals as well.

Your business is important and can be your path to wealth and security. But all the money and security in the world will not be any good if you do not have people to share it with. So work on your business but do it in moderation and take care of the rest of your life as well.

Integrating Recurring & Add-On Revenue

The difference between a good business and a really successful business lie within the products and services they sell. While making a profit on a sale is great for your business, generating repeat sales and recurring sales is what will take you and your business to the next level and beyond.

A business will find it very difficult to survive when they sell a products that people buy once or twice in their lifetime. These types of business have to constantly bring in new customers in order to make new sales. This is not only very hard to do but it is extremely costly as well. Doing business in this manner is a constant fight for attention and market share.

The best businesses are those businesses who sell products that people need and who are likely to purchase those products several times during their lives.

In addition, products that easily lend themselves to add-on or accessory sales are great for generating even more revenue and profits per sale. That is where the real money is often made.

Think about the difference in these two purchases:

A real estate agent will sell a home once to each customer. Maybe in a rare relationship they will sell a second home to that same person 10 years from now. Granted they made a huge profit on each sale but they still have to have a steady stream of new customers calling that agent for new home sales.

Contrast that to the store that sells bread and milk. Everyone uses bread and milk and similar products and not only do we use them on a daily basis but they only have a shelf life of two week tops. That means that we are going to purchase those products at least 25 times a year, probably more. There is less profit to be made on each purchase but we make many more purchases throughout the year.

Recurring revenue is the type of revenue that the business gets every month or year from their existing customers. These business pay the cost of acquiring the customer once and then get repeat business over and over until the customer either no longer needs the product or until they go somewhere else.

Think about the types of businesses that rely on recurring revenue for the majority of their income. Supermarkets, gas stations, clothing stores, home centers, doctors, dentists and the lists goes on and on. These are the type of products and sales that you need for your business.

Add-on sales are important too. Think about the person who goes into the store to buy that gallon of milk. While they are buying the milk they pick up eggs, butter, cereal, paper towel, a cake or dessert, meat for dinner, fruit, bakery items and a whole list of additional purchases! Often times the cost of the milk turns out to be the smaller part of the overall purchase!

The point I am trying to make here is that when you choose your business and product lines you should try to carry products that will result in multiple purchases over the course of every customer's life time as well as carry accessory items that will increase the amount of every sale. This will help you earn more money from every customer.

Think about it this way:

There is a certain cost for every new customer that walks through your doors. That customer either came as a result of advertising or promotion or because of word of mouth advertising from a previous or existing satisfied customer.

If you own an online business you pay a price for every visitor that visits your website whether they came from pay-per-click or other form of advertising. So the profit that is generated by each sale is reduced by the cost of getting that particular customer to come in to buy from you in the first place.

For example, if you place a $1,000 advertisement and it results in 100 people coming in and buying something from you, the cost of that customer acquisition would be roughly $10 per customer. It is actually a bit less because there probably would have been other customers who came in and were acquainted with your business but didn't buy anything that particular visit. But let's go with the $10 figure for simplicity sake.

So if each customer purchased something that gave your business a $15 profit, you actually only made a $5 profit because it costs you $10 to get the customer in. But when that same customer buys something else during that same visit, the full profit of that purchase goes to your business. Or, if that same customer comes back a week or so later to purchase something else, all of that profit goes to the business as well!

That is why so many new business struggle in the first months or year. They spend a lot of money just bringing customers through the doors that profits are much smaller than they are likely to be later on once the business had been established.

But if you can create recurring revenue to earn more and more from these new customers and if you can have all customers purchase additional add-on items then your profits will explode exponentially.

Even items that result in just one or two additional purchase during a customer's lifetime such as cars or appliances can benefit from add-on sales or recurring revenue sales. Car dealers sell extended warranties like appliance dealer do. They also sell oil changes and other maintenance services to add revenue.

In fact, there are many business models that make a great percentage, if not all, of their products just through recurring revenue and add-on sales. Be sure to create some of these revenue sources in your business to help it not only grow faster and become more profitable, but to help it become more self-sufficient and less reliant on constantly getting new customers for all of its new and pre-existing sales.

Creating a Scalable Business

One of the issues concerning some business relate to the size of the business being created and the size of the business the owner dreams of it becoming. While some of us would be happy with a small business in our local area catering to the general public while making a nice living, some people often dream about creating and owning the next Apple or Microsoft. While both options are sometimes achievable and possible, a lot depends on the type of business we create.

A large business is usually the result of a successful smaller business that is duplicated over and over in additional locations or the basic structure just increased to handle additional products and demand. Such a business is usually referred to as being "scalable".

Scalable means that you can easily take a $1 million dollar business and turn it into a $100 million dollar business by taking what has worked on a small scale and doing the same thing on a larger basis. Franchises are a perfect example of this but it can be done with other businesses as well.

For example, if you have the recipe for the world's best chocolate chip cookie and you opened a store selling them and it was a huge success, there stands no reason why you couldn't duplicate that same store in different cities across the nation or the world. After all, a great chocolate chip cookie in one town is still going to be good in another town as well. The only limitation would be the ability to create as many cookies as needed to make the demand. But there are bakers and kitchens able to do that all over so that should not be an issue.

But let's say that you have a product that depends heavily on your presence or skills to create it. Maybe you have an art gallery where you make a great living selling your paintings. But to grow that business to a business that had 100 locations would require you to paint 100 times more paintings and that would be almost impossible. While you might sell prints or reproductions, you could not sell the most popular originals.

You also could not hire additional artists because they are not likely to have the same exact talents or capabilities that you have. Their pictures would look better and have a different feel to them. Because of this you would have a nice and successful business in your area and possibly online but it would not be considered scalable.

If you are selling products made or manufactured by others, or if you provide services that are easily trained and duplicated elsewhere, those would be considered scalable business as well. As long as the supply of product was sufficient you could expand your business to any size you desire.

So when you are planning your business, give some thought to where you would like to take your business. If you will be happy with a smaller or more localized business, then plan accordingly and with those parameters in mind. But if you are looking to build the next business kingdom or dominant force, keep scalability in mind and focus on delivering the products and services that lend themselves best to that business model.

Also keep in mind that the larger your business gets the more people you are going to have to hire, supervise and be responsible for. If you can find the right people your business can explode and do very well. But if you hire the wrong people, they could do more harm than good for your entire business. It is best to always remember that as you expand your business.

Creating a Stable
& Secure Business

This chapter might make a few of you a little bit scared and this is not my intent/ But you need to be aware of one very important thing when it comes to the overall success of your business. That one thing is taking steps to insure a steady stream of products to sell to your customers.

Unless you manufacture or make your own products and services, you are at least partially vulnerable to the supplier of the products you sell. You could invest a ton of time and money in building a successful business based around one or two products and then have the whole thing come crashing down when those products are taken away from your business.

For this reason I always encourage people to build their businesses around an entire selection of products from different manufacturers and vendors. This way your business might be hurt by the absence of one or two products but not be crippled or devastated by that happening to you one product.

We should establish relationships with several suppliers so that should one of them go out of business or refuse to sell to us we have other people to turn to. When we have other sources these changes or problems are never impacting our customers. That is always the desired result. Things happen every day in business and changes have to be made and dealt with. But as long as we keep these changes and problems invisible to the customer there is little damage to the business.

People who have exclusive rights or a monopoly on a single product are the most dangerous. Unless you have a contract with them they can raise the price without notice, refuse to sell to you unless you make certain concessions and put your business through all sorts of hell in the process. Even if you have a contract by the time you go through the legal system your business could be out of business and you would lose a ton of money fighting what happened. Even a victory in court would be a hollow victory.

Always have several sources for anything you need to sustain your business. Do not deal with just one supplier or service provider as that will leave you vulnerable to the actions of others that could seriously damage or impact your business.

The same also holds true if your business is selling your products to other businesses.

If you are a manufacturer you should try to diversify your customer base so that most of your sales are to a large number of other businesses or customers. If you sell exclusively to one or two main customers then they will be able to dictate to your business the terms of their purchases.

Business is a cut throat process and once a company sees that they have another company extremely dependent upon their business they will usually act to get better pricing or other concessions from that business. If this is your main customer and their sales are crucial to your business then you will be pressured to agree to those terms or place your business at risk.

Make no mistake about it though, when major retailers approach your business with an extremely large or this can be enticing. And I am not telling you to turn that order away. But I am warning you against granting anyone exclusivity to any of your products because once you do you eliminate others from also making potentially better offers in the future.

If you are faced with such an offer I strongly urge you to contact your accountant and your lawyer before signing anything. They will advise you about whether or not this offer is good for your business and what the details really are in the contract.

So of these documents are so confusing and full of legal jargon that it is easy for the novice business owner to miss a potentially deadly phrase or condition that can change everything. Always consult with your attorney or lawyer.

When you are setting up your business and as you are growing it, always keep your options open when it comes to where you sell and purchase products. Always have a back-up plan in place should any vendor or provider go out of business or if the relationship should change for whatever reason.

Keep a list of all possible suppliers of the products you sell and of the companies who provide the critical services you needs as well. Always investigate new potential partners and sources so if trouble should occur, you will know right away where and who you should go to seek relief. Doing this in advance enables you to avoid the searching and lost time that other will experience when problems occur in their business. Plus, you might just find a better source for things your business needs than you have now.

Your end goals should be to have a business that is capable of handling any issue or problem without anything being noticed by the customers or without having the customers impacted in any way. This will help your business weather any problem and keep it healthy, growing and successful at the same time.

Diversification

Much along the same lines as developing a safe and secure business, diversifying your business into many areas is something that we should all consider once we have our core business set up and running well. Diversification is something that will help our business survive as the marketplace changes around us.

For those business owners out there who think that their product is perfect and will always be in demand, I would politely ask them to think again. For those of you who think that your business will do just fine with one or two core products, I will also ask you to think again as well. And for those of you who fall into both categories, and even if you just fall into one, I will ask you to do just one thing.

Take a minute to talk to any of the thousands of people who owned successful video rental stores in the 1980's and 1990's. If you can even find one of them still in business today.

In the 80's and 90's video stores were all the rage and they were popping up all over every town in the country. You had 5 or 6 in every town and opening one was pretty much a guarantee of becoming successful. Now 20-30 years later, I dare you to try and find one video store. Sure you can rent DVD's but they usually come from a machine inside a supermarket or drug store.

Business is very much a cyclical process where things go in and out of style and demand frequently. Plus, if something is successful, copycats pop up all over looking to get into the lucrative market, make a fast buck and then get out. Lastly, automation has made it possible to accomplish many tasks by machines instead of businesses and people. The DVD rental kiosk is the perfect example of automation replacing a brick and mortar store.

Fortunately, most trends do not disappear overnight. You do not go from selling 10,000 of something one week to selling 4 the next. It is usually a gradual process that may or may not go very fast. What this means is that the smart business owner will look for new products to take the place of older products that might be approaching the end of the lifespan in the marketplace.

This doesn't mean the new products will take the place of the old products because there still might be a continual demand for them on some level.

But it does mean that the new products will be there to boost the sales of the business as older products sell less. This helps insure a constant level of total sales for the business.

A good business owner concerns him or herself with not just total sales but sales of each product they sell. This way we can spot trends early on and also understand what it is our customers are looking for. This helps us decide which products to carry and how to properly choose the products we sell.

Though this is a vast oversimplification, we should be carrying more of the products that sell well and less of the products that sell poorly. It is a simple concept but one that is sometimes difficult to follow. That is because it requires time, effort and a bit of analysis in order to make the right decisions.

There are two objectives when it comes to protecting your business and making it future-proof. Both require constant attention and analysis. It is not difficult and it is also not that time-consuming once you get in the habit and keep up with what is going on with your business.

We want to spot trends and be able to take advantage of those trends as they occur.

That means identifying them early in the process so there is still money to be made and it means scaling down on items when they enter the end or training part of the trend, People or businesses who get into a trend too late might purchase heavily at the time when those items are on the way out.

You can spot trends in a few different ways. Here are a few ways to see which trends are affecting your business or industry:

Listen to Your Customers

Sometimes our best source of information comes from the people who purchase our existing products. If several people ask if you carry the same new product, consider looking into the product to see what it is all about. If this is something that is just catching on, you might want to consider handling it.

For example, over 50 years ago someone walked into a record store and asked the owner if they had a certain record by this unknown group called The Beatles. If didn't but looked into it and started stocking the record. I think that probably worked out well for him, don't you think?

Listening to what people are saying or talking about can give you a heads up on what is selling now or what the next big thing is going to be. It doesn't cost anything other than time to listen so you should give it a try.

Read Industry or Trade Publications

While I understand that reading trade publications is not the most exciting or thrilling reading, there is a lot of information to be gained by doing so. One thing these publications are good for is identifying new trends and alerting members as to what they should be selling at any given time. While you have to be careful and be able to recognize legitimate information from a disguised sales pitch, you can get some very insightful information from these sources.

The other benefit of trade publication is that you can read about what is happening all over the world. Since trends usually start in one place and get big there first, you can often get a head start on the next new thing by reading about what is happening across the country or the globe. This way you can prepare for when it reaches your area. While others are just learning about something, you can be ready!

Watch the News

The evening news programs often will have stories on what is happening elsewhere and what new things are on the horizon. Sometimes you get a glimpse of something new long before anyone else. Then you can look into it a little more to see if this is something that might be of use to you or your business.

Watch for On-Line Trending

Today the internet is a huge source of information on just about everything. One of the most useful things you can do is search Google and Yahoo for what is currently trending or what is new. Just a few simple searches could very well give you several products or services that are going to be the next new thing.

Sometimes it is just not your business that needs to be diversified but the entire industry that you function or sell within. That means that some of us will be owning businesses that just might have a limited life span. Getting back to that video store example we already used, if you had a store in that industry after a while you would have seen the writing on the wall and would have either transformed your business into something else or perhaps sold your business while it was still worth something.

If you look at the most successful businesses that have been around for decades and you will see that virtually every one of them are selling different products today than they did 30 or 40 years ago. They are selling different products, a wider variety of products and they are constantly adapting to what people in their area want or are looking for.

That is the way businesses survive. That is the way businesses make it through changes in the marketplace.

Business become pro-active and learn what to do now so that they are prepared for later. It is not all that hard but it requires patience and effort. If you are one of those business owners who is content to keep your now successful business just like it is, you might find yourself turning into one of those ex-business owners who wondered why their business failed.

Becoming Known
(Developing Your Brand)

At this point you now have your business plan all set-up and have brought your business all the way from a dream or concept into an honest to goodness reality. So now that you have your business ready to go and your doors open, we now have to start out becoming known in your community or on-line depending on which type of business you have created.

Somewhere in your business plan should have how you wanted to be thought of or perceived by the general public. That is how your brand is going to be thought of by the people who purchase your products. All your marketing and promotion should be designed to strengthen and support your brand image.

For example, if your business is focused on selling merchandise at the lowest prices, then your advertising and marketing should revolve around the low cost concept. You can include other things such as high quality and huge selection but the driving force or message behind everything centers on low prices.

But if your business is designed as a one stop resource for your customers, which is common for specialty stores or stores that sell just one type of product, then your advertising and marketing should stress that you are the one main resource for anything and everything to do with the type of product you are selling. Price can be a part of things but it would not be the primary focus.

Your brand needs to stand for something and create a mental picture or image in the mind of the customer. Your "brand" should be as close to that mental image or picture as possible otherwise you will not get the customer recognition or understanding that you are going to need.

Your business also needs to reinforce your brand as well. You cannot advertise one thing and then deliver something else. If someone comes in expecting to find low priced merchandise but finds high end products at inflated prices, they will be confused and even angry. If you market your store as the local resource for certain types of products yet your sales people do not have the knowledge to answer even basic questions, then your business will not support your brand.

In short, your "brand" is going to be what you present and offer to your customers. Understanding this is the first part of building that particular brand and showcasing it to customers.

Your end goal is to have your business name become synonymous with what you want your business to represent.

For example, if you open a new business and name it after your last name and call it "Smith's", in the beginning no one is going to know what "Smith's" really is. But after you market your business and advertise it and become known by people in your area, the name "Smith's" will soon become a brand and people will think about your products and services when they hear the name "Smiths"

For example, if I were to ask you if you want to go to McDonalds, almost everyone would know we were going to get a burger or some French fries. That's because the name "McDonalds" has developed a strong worldwide brand as a fast food hamburger place. That is because everything they do and everything the market supports their brand perfectly.

You need to treat your brand very carefully and develop it carefully as well. EVERYTHING you do in your business should be carefully designed to support or enhance your brand. Every product you sell and every action you take should be designed to make your brand better and more powerful. This stands for everything you do involving your business.

One of the most important questions a business owner needs to ask him or herself every time they are doing anything should be:

"Does what I'm doing enhance or damage my brand?"

If it enhances your brand then you should continue. But if it damages your brand, or makes your brand confusing to the customer, then you should reconsider. Your goal is to create a powerful and distinctive brand so that when customers think of the brand they think of you.

You can carry other products and diversify to a certain extent but you must always be committed to your core brand. For example, McDonalds sells salads but it is still known primarily as a hamburger restaurant. Adding salads makes it more desirable for certain people but its core brand is still enhanced by adding the salads.

Be careful when designing your brand as well because it is difficult to change your brand once you have started. Trying to change a brand takes time and money and also introduces a lot of confusion in the minds of customers throughout the process. But once you have your brand established, you need to market your brand to the right people.

Hopefully in your planning and starting practice you did some research and found that there is indeed a market for the brand you are creating and the products that you are selling.

If you have done that research and have established that a need already exists, then at the same time you have also identified the people who are most likely to need the products you are selling.

These are the same people you are now going to have to market your new business to. After all, doesn't it make sense to market your business to the same people you have already established need your products and services? Of course it does! So now that you know who need what you are selling, you need to find out how to reach those people effectively and inexpensively.

We are going to target the publications and newspapers and magazines that our target group of people are most likely to read or watch. If our products are geared towards children then we are going to advertise in places that children go, watch or read. The same for adults. We are going to pick the magazines that our target audience is likely to read and we will avoid, at first, those papers and publications where they are not likely to read.

Then, as these new customers walk through the doors or visit our website, we are going to have to be careful to provide them with an experience that is appropriate for the business model and brand we have created.

If we are creating a brand known for expertise and quality we are going to make sure we have high quality products and sales people well trained so that they can provide assistance and advice to your customers. We are going to make sure that we have people available who can answer specific questions, solve specific problems and help the customer get the most they possibly can from their purchase. This is important because you want to be known as the place to go when people have problems and questions. So if this is what you want your business to become known for, you need to have the employees and business structure to support it.

A brand usually consists of several different parts. If you want to create a powerful brand you are going to have to create a business that hits as many of those parts as possible. Going back to the fast food example, people expect lower prices, faster service and a uniform experience no matter which location a customer goes to for their food. If the lines are long and the service is slow and the prices are higher, the brand is going to suffer.

That is why there are so many rules and procedures that franchisees must follow to stay in business. It is not so much to protect the franchisee as it is to protect the brand. In order for the brand to stay strong, it has to be supported well.

That means having everyone doing things the same way so the same customers continue to get the same experience every time in every location.

So in your business, make sure you have the proper rules, procedures and processes in place to support your brand and your business. That means training employees in how to treat customers and how to support your brand. It means everyone in the business understanding what your brand is and then living up to that brand. As your brand grows so does your business.

Last but not least, there is one more important thing to remember when it comes to your brand. Much like a reputation, a brand takes a long time to establish and a very short time to destroy. That is why it is so important to always do and say the things required to enhance your brand and staying far away from those things that can destroy it. You can wipe out years of good-will and brand recognition with just one bad experience. While mistakes are bound to happen to even the best of us, we must take as many precautions as possible to avoid damaging our brand at all costs.

Customer Service

When it comes to virtually every successful business, there is one aspect of the business that is usually top-notch. That part of the business is their customer service. It is how they treat the people that come in and buy their products and services. Because without customers, there is no business that can survive.

Every single business, without exception, needs customer to purchase their products and services. Unless you are a monopoly, like the government, or unless only you manufacture and sell a particular product, you are going to have to compete against other business for your customers. That means that you are going to have to supply a reasonably good overall customer experience for your customers.

Today there is more competition than ever before when it comes to just about every business. In the past we would have to deal with competition on a local level. Just a few stores with a several miles of where our business was located.

After all, people love convenience and there would have to be a powerful reason to go out of one's way when there was a more convenient option.

But now with almost everyone having a computer or a smart phone, we have to contend with competition not only within our local area but all over the country and in some cases, even the world! Just a few clicks on a mouse or a few taps on a phone screen can allow us to search for in a few minutes what used to take us days to seek out!

But all of this competition also brings us more opportunity as well. In the past we would have to settle for those people who lived near us while today, that same technology that brought us more competition now also brings us a ton more customers from all over the globe! So along with the bad also comes a great deal of good!

So you might be wondering right about now what all of this has to do with customer service. Well, the more options a customer has, the more "picky" or demanding that customer can be. When you have only one or two options when it comes to where you purchase you are pretty much dictated to by the vendor. But when you have 5, 10 or more options you can go wherever you want and search out who offers you the best overall value.

Since customer service is a critical part of the buying process, you need to excel at customer service to keep your customers coming back for more. Customer service is a very complex process and we have written entire books on the customer service process. But for the purposes of this book, we will give you a condensed version as far as what you have to offer the customer to keep them happy and coming back for more.

Value

While price is not the only factor when it comes to the overall value of doing business with you, it does usually play a significant role. But customers are also usually willing to pay more for superior service, selection and overall value. In fact, some stores are able to charge premium prices and still get people to come back again and again because of the way they are treated.

Appreciation

Customers are people just like you and I and everyone likes to feel appreciated. If we treat our customers like they are a bother or an interruption to what we are doing at the time, they will not feel appreciated and are far more likely to leave and go somewhere else.

It doesn't take long to say "hello" and "thank you" or "How can we help you today" all with a smile on our faces as we say it. But it is amazing how many business treat their customers like they feel it is a privilege to allow them to do business with you. If you want to drive customers away, don't make them feel needed or appreciated.

Problem Solving

All customers have problems of one kind or another that they come to you to have resolved. It might be the need for a specific product or it could be a problem with an existing product. Whatever their problems might be, they are looking to you and your business to resolve them and you need to be able to do just that every time.

Problem solving lies at the heart of a great many purchases. We pay our hard earned money to buy a product that will do something for us or make it easier and better to do it ourselves. Just as important are the services and problem solving your business is expected to do for your customers. So whether it is a simple exchange, defective return or just a question on how to go about doing something, your customers are looking for you to provide the answers and to solve their problems.

It is important to understand that even a small problem can become a bigger one very fast if you don't say or do the right thing.

Customer Service Training teaches us to place ourselves in the position of the customer and to realize how the customer feels in this particular situation. That way we can emphasize with how they feel and proceed accordingly.

Convenience

We are a busy society and few people have a lot of excess time that they can use to wait around or just take longer to do things. Because of this we must make it as easy as possible for anyone to do business with us. That means providing fast service, make products easier to locate in our store or website and in the case of brick and mortar stores, having hours that make it easy for people to shop within their busy schedules.

People like to get in, get what they want and get out all in the fastest period of time possible. But at the same time they also demand access to information and assistance when they need it. So your business has to be there on the first lines to give the customer what they need when they need it. And you must do it quickly.

Empathy

Customers also like it when a business appears to care about their needs and problems.

Customers love it when businesses show that they are emotionally involved in the customer's problems. While they do not have to admit responsibility to the customer for their problems, they can show empathy towards the customer.

Empathy means letting the customer know you are truly sorry that they are having this problem and that you feel their pain as well. It means letting them know that you are going to try your best to resolve their problem. You are not necessarily taking responsibility or admitting guilt, you are just showing the customer that you care. That is a big difference.

Just saying something like "I am sorry that you are having this problem. Let me see what I can do to help resolve it for you." does not show or express guilt. It just shows you care. You could follow up that statement with something like "The problems is that you used the wrong setting. If you use setting 5 you should be good to go. Only use setting 3 for light duty tasks."

This nicely tells the customer there is no defect and that it was operator error while not placing or assigning any blame. It also shows the customer you care because you spent the time and made the effort to show them how to solve the problem moving forward. Most of the time all the customer wants is a show of empathy and a resolution made available to them.

Word of Mouth – Both Good & Bad

Here is the one part of customer service that is often a great unknown. Part of taking care of existing customers is so they will speak highly about your business to others. These other people might include friends, co-workers, family members and other people they might come in contact with throughout the rest of their daily lives.

The unknown part is exactly how many people each customer might tell. Are they going to tell 5 people or 50? Maybe even 500 if they have the opportunity. We never know who they will tell of how many people will be told.

The one thing we do know is that the stronger the reaction, either both positive or negative, the more people will be told because the impression was that much stronger. So if we go above and beyond and provide an amazing customer experience, we can expect a lot more positive comments made to other people. If we do the expected, or provide an experience that the customer thought they should receive, we would probably not get much positive word of mouth comments because no real impression was made.

But when we really anger or annoy a customer, we can almost always count on much more negative commentary to a lot more people.

That is because people like to inform other people about negative experiences so as to protect them from experiencing the same things themselves. Some studies have shown that angry customers will tell more than 5 times more people than satisfied customers will so that can be a real problem.

Even more important is how many of those people are in turn going to tell even more people. If the experience is good or bad enough or really unusual, the response and associated comments could quickly "go viral". This may or may not happen but you will never be able to know with any degree of certainty what is going to happen.

We also do not know what kind or how much business each of those people might represent. Some will but more or less than others and sometimes we might miss out on huge purchases that might come from people we don't even know who were influenced one way or another by the comments and experiences of others. So we might have lost $100 or $100, 000,000 of business and we would never know.

A lot of business owner reject incurring the expense of training their people in customer service techniques because it is impossible to attach an accurate number to their return on investment. For people with a black and white type of analytical personality, they will not spend money on anything that cannot be proven.

For example, if you go to a business owner and tell them that if they spend $1,000 they will definitely earn $10,000 in extra sales, and if you have enough factual data to back up those claims, most business owners would gladly agree to spend the $1,000. Or at least test the market with a smaller investment.

But try to convince that same business owner that if he spent $1,000 that he might increase sales or save the company $10,000 and that you could not provide them with any specific data on your claims, and you would have a much more difficult time closing the sale. This is one of the chief roadblocks when trying to get businesses to train their people in customer service.

But the facts remain that providing the best customer service experience to your customers is the best way to keep your customers happy. It can cost more than 10 times more to bring a new customer through the doors than it does to keep an existing customer happy. So it not only makes sense to spend that money and improve the customer experience it is financially smart to do so as well.

Customer service is by nature a reactive process in most companies and those companies spend more time putting out fires and resolving problems than they do making things better for the customer.

While problem resolution is an important part of any business, the best method by far to improving customer service is by solving problems before they even get to the customer level.

That means creating a customer focused business where every rule, policy and procedure is both customer friendly and business friendly. It means being respectful and aware of customer issues and doing your best to resolve problems as early in the process as possible. That means always taking the customer's need into consider and doing everything possible to create the best customer experience.

This also means having the right products in stock the majority of the time and be able to deliver those products quickly as well. We also live in a world full of instant gratification and people today do not like to wait for the things they want. So you better have it in stock and you better be able to deliver it to them quickly or they will find someone else who can.

It is also important to once again go over the fact that customer service is part of everyone's job in the company. If a problem anywhere along the line is not resolved properly the entire customer experience is damaged. So when it comes to training people on customer service, do not just train one or two people or just one department. Train everyone so that everyone is on the same page and knows what to do in every situation for every customer.

Companies have built stellar reputations on their customer service and this has allowed them to thrive while other businesses just survive and also help them charge premium prices when other business have to cut prices to the core just to complete a sale.

Great customer service is something that can either make or break a business. The good news is that providing great customer service is very easy once you adapt a customer focused business. Once the attitude is generated and the proper policies and procedures put in place, the rest just runs on auto-pilot as long as everyone is one the same page.

It's very easy to do but yet for some reason so many business just don't seem to bother doing it. Which is great for you because if you do things right eventually their customers will become your customers!

And when that happens, don't shed a single tear for them. They had their chance and they blew it.

Now don't blow yours.

Legal Issues

Right from the beginning let me say that we are not lawyers and we are not pretending that we are at least remotely qualified to give you correct and detailed legal information or guidance. That is why every business of any size should have a lawyer they can turn to while setting up their business and then as they are running it. Qualified legal representation is not a luxury, it is a necessity.

Though it is a shame to say, we live in a society where a certain segment of the population is always looking for ways to get ahead in life at the expense of someone else. We have frivolous lawsuits, nuisance lawsuits, bogus claims and all other kinds of nonsense that are becoming more and more common for most businesses. So we are going to need the help of a qualified legal expert from time to time.

If you have one, use them. If you don't have one, find one. Find one now!

Pay attention to your lawyer and your accountant to make sure that you are in compliance with all the rules and regulations pertaining to you and your business. If you own a store make sure everything in your store is up to code. Make sure there are no hazards or anything in your store that is dangerous or in any way unsafe.

If there is anything that is even in doubt, correct it now before it becomes a lawsuit. Because stuff happens and eventually it is going to happen to you. When something does happen, you want to make as sure as possible that it was not through your negligence.

The same holds true for online businesses as well. Make sure your website conforms to the applicable legal standards including the proper disclaimers and other information required on your website by law. Ignorance is no defense. If you are in violation of anything, take care of it now before someone spots the violation.

Though it needs to explanation, of course you should conduct your business in an honest and open manner with no false or misleading advertising. Make no false claims or exaggerated claims when it comes to what your products can do or can't do. It is better to lose a sale than find yourself in a court of law.

Make sure your business has the appropriate type and amounts of insurance to protect you when stuff does happen. Even a small lawsuit can place a business in bankruptcy today if you don't have insurance. Talk to your accountant to make sure you have enough insurance. Your lawyer can also advise you on the types of insurance you need as well. You can also ask your insurance agent but always remember that they are paid to sell you insurance so their recommendations are not always 100% honest!

When problems do happen, and they will eventually, do the right thing and do what's right. If you made a mistake, take responsibility for it. Do not hide behind the law and do not use loopholes and vague wording to escape from doing the right thing. Trust me when I say that word will get around if you try to run an unethical or scam type business. Remember, once you damage your brand, it may never be the same again. So be very careful.

To help isolate your personal possessions and finances from your business make sure to work with your lawyer and accountant to set up the right kind of business so your home, cars and other possession may be shielded from a business problem or lawsuit. If is better to be safe up-front than sorry later on.

Also keep in mind that you are not only responsible for your actions but also for the actions of your employees as well.

They represent your business and they can cause you a lot of problems by saying or doing the wrong thing at the wrong time to the wrong person. Make sure everyone is educated on how you want things done. Make sure people know when to escalate situations to you so that you can take over and make the right decisions. This alone can save you a lot of headaches down the road.

Basically we suggest you get a good lawyer and listen to their advice. Run an open and honest business where you make every effort to do the right thing and do right by your customer. Stand behind what you sell and make things right when customers have problems. You will not only get a great reputation you will also be covering yourself well should legal action follow.

This is because your actions now will be scrutinized later by lawyers and possibly a judge and a jury. When they see a businessman trying to do what's right but still having trouble with a customer, it will look better for the business when everyone sees the steps you took to do whatever you could that was right. Anything you can do in those situations to show an honest attempt to resolve the problem will help your case in the eyes of a judge and/or jury.

Always consult your lawyer before making any major decisions and involve your accountant to make sure those decisions make financial sense as well. If there is any time that you are not sure what to do, I advise playing it safe and doing more than you are required under the law. If you take this route you can never be accused of being anti-customer or trying to circumvent the law.

Sometimes perception can be very powerful and if the perception is that you went out of the way or over and above to help a customer that might be all you need to emerge victorious from a legal problem.

Tax Issues

The other issues that involve any business whether a brand new one or a long existing one are tax issues and financial issues. Most of the time both are tangled up with each other and are addressed as one. When you have tax or financial issues, the one person you need to involve is your accountant. Engage your accountant first and then your lawyer if needed second. Do not expect a lawyer to make financial decisions for you or your accountant to make legal decisions. Neither are qualified to act for the other.

The most important aspect of taxes when it comes to businesses are knowing what taxes need to be paid and when each tax is due. Not all taxes are due on April 15th. Some must be paid several times a year while others might have their own separate deadlines. Ignorance is no excuse and you must be aware of what needs to be paid and when the payment is due.

Though your accountant will help you make sure everything is done right and done on time, the responsibility lies with you, the business owner, NOT your accountant. If you miss a payment or do not file at all the State or IRS will come after YOU and YOUR business NOT your accountant. So make sure your accountant is doing what they are supposed to and make sure all payments are being made properly and on time.

Which brings up an interesting point.

While you do not have to be a legal or financial expert, you do need to have a basic understanding of what needs to be done, how it needs to be done and when it needs to be done. You also need to understand how to do it and why it makes sense and why it is required. This is important because at times you might be asked questions as to why something was done that way or someone might question why you did what you did and you must be able to understand.

There have been many times where accountants and lawyer have mislead business owners and claimed to have made the required payments or filed the appropriate forms when in fact they never did either of those things. This could go on for years until the authorities come after the business for non-payment. Then the business owner is caught unaware and has no idea what happened to cause these problems.

Because of this, the business owner should work WITH their accountant and go over every form and ask as many questions as possible so they have a thorough understanding of what is being submitted. They should ask to see cancelled checks, receipts for payment and any other form paperwork or correspondence from any government or financial institution.

You should also be aware of every deduction and entry on the forms as well. This is because some accountants might overstate deductions and understate income so you get a larger refund. The accountant might do this so the client is happy and has to pay less taxes. While everyone does this to some minor extent, should you get audited it is your business that is on the line not the accountant or person who prepared your forms for you. You will be the one looking at fines and possible jail time. While they might go after the accountant later, they will come after you first and again, ignorance is no excuse.

Choose your accountant carefully and make sure they are experienced in the type and size business you are running now and hopefully will grow into later. Not all areas of accounting are the same and just like there are different types of lawyers there are different types of accountants as well. Take your time and make your choice wisely.

Local Rules & Regulations

Here is one area where most business owners have to go it alone with help only from their accountant and lawyer. Every area has its own regulations and requirements when it comes to businesses. It is up to the business owner to make sure that they are in total compliance at all times when they are in business. Failure to be in compliance will often be met with fines and possible suspension of your business.

In most areas there will be certain types of business that require a license to perform that type of service or to sell products in that area. This is done to protect consumers against scam artists and frauds although a major reason for these licenses is also the revenue they generate. In some cases all you need to do is pay a fee and show proof of insurance while for other licenses you may have to pass a test that is designed to demonstrate knowledge and competency.

If you provide any type of service you might have to be bonded or have a minimum amount of insurance to protect yourself against damage claims or from performing poor quality work. The actual amount of insurance may vary depending on the type of business and the services you perform. Failure to have enough insurance or the right type of insurance will result in your business being out of compliance and you can have your license revoked or suspended. There will probably be fines incurred as well.

Beware that many licenses and permits cover only a certain geographical area and you might be permitted to do work in one part of town and not in another. So the reality is that you might have to have several licenses depending on the work you do and the areas you will cover. You should only do work in the areas where you are licensed. Otherwise you could be in line for fines and other disciplinary action.

You should check with your local consumer affairs office and/or government offices for the requirements to open a business in your home town. You might have to formally register a business name and show proof of insurance and other items in order to register your chosen name. Follow their instructions to the letter to make sure there are no mistakes which could result in lost time or income.

You also might have to register with the state and federal governments as well depending on the type of business you are opening. Your lawyer and accountant can help advise you on these areas which may vary widely from one are to another. It is best to get everything you need in the beginning so you will not have projects or work held up later because you are not properly licensed.

Because there are so many different rules and regulations depending on where you live and because so many of these vary widely in both scope and requirements, I urge everyone to ask their local government or business agency for a book on local business regulations. This can help you make sure you are in compliance and remain there.

Also keep in mind that it is your responsibility to keep up with the rules and regulations pertaining to your business at all times. These rules do change and it is up to you to know when they change and what now is required for your business. Ignorance is no excuse and while there might be a grace period that allows you time to get in compliance it is always best to make the changes sooner rather than later.

Joining a local business group or organization is a great way of finding out what is happening and how it could effect your business. Not only that but the contacts you make could help you in other areas of your business as well.

So join a couple of organizations to make sure you remain informed and also to start your network.

This is one area where you cannot afford to be lax or lazy. Fines can be substantial and even result in the loss of your business. Keep meticulous records in case they should be asked for and always operate your business within the rules of regulations of your local area. Failure to do so can result in the loss of your license and in some case even make the papers which will be publicity for your business you definitely do not need or want.

Networking

Even the smallest of business run by a single person is not a single person operation. There are always other people involved in the business such as vendors, suppliers, advertisers and marketing people. All of these parts of your business are important and it makes sense to make as many contacts and become as widely known as possible in your area or online depending on what type of business you are starting.

Networking is the process of introducing yourself to the people and companies in your industry and local area. You want to do this for several reasons. First of all, as a new business owner looking to establish your business, you need to get your business out in front of as many people as possible. Not so much to generate sales but to generate awareness of your business and the products it sells.

Second, as a business owner you are going to need relationships with other people to get your business to the next level.

You want to get to know other business owners so that you can learn from them and vice versa. Plus, you are going to need help at times and might just be looking for a strategic partner for a venture down the road.

People like to do business with people that they know. With so many shysters and scammers out there today that are looking to make as much as they can while providing the least amount of value, personal relationships and recommendations are the lifeblood of every new and established business.

People used to use something called a Rolodex which was a rotating card file with all their contacts on it. Then, when they needed something or someone for a particular purpose all they had to do was search through their rolodex for that particular person. Then they would find someone they either knew or had heard about via a personal recommendation and they already had a certain comfort level with that company or individual.

Many people confuse networking with making sales and while networking does lead to sales it is not a one stop process. Networking leads to familiarity. Familiarity leads to confidence. Confidence leads to a recommendation and finally these recommendations lead to sales.

It is a multi-step process rather than something immediately leading to a sale. While sometimes this does and can happen, usually it takes time.

People sometimes make the mistake of meeting someone for the first time and immediately hitting them with a sales pitch. Or they join a business organization and immediately start pushing their business to the members at their first meeting. This not only doesn't work all that well it actually turns people and other businesses off and will do more harm than good for your business.

Instead, you join an organization and get involved with that organization. Let people know that you own a business and what that business sells or does but stop right there. Work within the organization to help it achieve its goals and if there is a role for you and your business then sponsor an event or volunteer your business or services. This is how you get to be known as a valued business in the community.

For example, you own a catering company and you join the local business association. You attend meetings and when you hear about an upcoming event, you could volunteer to do the catering either for free or at cost. Your business gets publicity, people taste your food and experience you service and if your business does well, you walk away with brand and name recognition as well as possibly a few leads.

But networking is more than just generating business or sales. Networking puts you in touch with people and businesses that can help your business grow and succeed as well. Through your contacts you might meet a great graphics artist or a great website designer. Or you might have people referred to you for a job by people who can vouch for the character and abilities of that individual.

Who do you think would be the safest and best hire? Someone who does really good at interviews but performs lousy when they get the job because their resume was pure fiction and they just practiced how to ace an interview or someone who came with a personal recommendation from someone you knew and trusted?

99% of the time the person with the personal recommendation will be the better and safest choice. After all, no one is going to recommend a loser to someone they have a relationship with! You still have to do your due diligence and make sure the person fits your company but that personal recommendation carries a ton of weight when it comes to making a decision.

The same works for companies as well. If you need a great fulfillment company, your networking might make you aware of a company that you otherwise might never had become aware of.

Everyone networks for a reason and most of the reason is awareness. The more people that know you the more people who might possibly know you and need your services.

That is the beauty of networking when it is done right. Everyone benefits in two ways. First they get recognized and their business gets recognized. The more people that know about your business and what it does the more people who might need what you sell and come to you the next time they need to buy someone.

But at the same time people learn about you, you also are learning about them. So you now have people you know for when it comes time that you might need something for your business. It is a give and take process where both people benefit.

The other great thing about marketing is that while you get to know a lot of great people and businesses you also at the same time learn about the really bad people and businesses as well. Sometimes this is more important than finding the great ones because a bad employee or business can do irreparable harm to your business very quickly. But when you network and join organizations, you get the "head's up" on the really bad or poor businesses right away.

To be fair we should warn you that networking is a lot of work especially in the beginning. When you first start you know no one and no one knows you.

There will be hesitancy and maybe a little wariness or suspicion in the beginning as people get to know you and try to figure out if you are one of the good people or one of the bad guys. That is why it is so important to provide the best impression in the beginning and not push your agenda at the very beginning. Let people get to know you before they get to know your business.

This is important because a good person will usually run a good and legitimate business. A creep is more likely to be the scammer that gets a quick buck and then is never heard from again. So let people get comfortable with you and they will soon be receptive to your business as well.

But networking gets easier as more people get to know you and really takes off when people who know you start recommending you and your business to others. That is when you start getting calls and leads and sales and when your networking really starts to pay off. This is when marketing really starts to get easier and more rewarding.

Don't underestimate the value in networking. Don't think it is too much time or not valuable enough.

It is hard to run a successful business all by yourself regardless of what kind of business you are in. there is so much going on in every industry and every local area that networking actually becomes an invaluable source of information and guidance and it comes to you and your business for free!

Looking at networking in that lights will probably make you rethink the value of effective marketing. Just remember to take it slow, do it right and give people the right impression of you and your business. Once you are able to do that, the rest is very easy and even more effective.

Hiring Employees

One of the most scary, even frightening parts of starting a new business is hiring employees. While it is sometimes possible to run an entire business by yourself, there are only so many hours in a week that one person can work. So unless your business is an internet based business that is mostly automated, one person just isn't going to cut it.

Plus, even if you could fulfill all the needs of your business and even if you were able to stay awake on very little sleep and work 20 hours days, there are several reasons why this is just not reasonable or even effective.

First of all, as we have already mentioned, there is just no way that one person can be effective and the best at everything that goes into creating and running a successful business. While we might be able to put in the time, our skills are usually going to be less than others when it comes to at least a few things that are needed for our business.

So even if we had the time to do everything ourselves, we wouldn't do a very good job.

Second, when we spend time doing less valuable things that still need to be done, we are taking away time from our strengths and using that time in less valuable ways. We are usually much better off doing what we do best and what has the most value to our business instead of trying to be the jack of all trades. Dedicating our time to where it has the most value and impact will help our business grow faster and better.

Third, no matter how dedicated and serious we might be about our business, we can only work long hours for a limited amount of time. After that time passes we become burnt out and our productivity goes way down and our results go down with it. Plus, the rest of our life, which has been neglected for so long as we worked on our business is not in shambles as well. All of that can lead to fatigue and sometimes depression.

So let's just skip ahead and all agree that at some point, we are going to have to hire employees. Not a whole bunch but at least one or two or a few to cover schedules and fulfill all the skills sets that our business requires. It's not a question of should you hire employees it is instead a question of how many and what do you need them to do.

Before we go about interviewing employees, we need to determine as exactly as possible what we want, expect and need from the employees we are going to hire. After all, we cannot expect to find and hire the perfect employee unless we know what the perfect employee looks like when it comes to our business.

Here are a few things to consider before hiring any employees:

What Skills Sets are you Looking for?

This might seem a bit silly to state this but not every employee is going to need or use the same skills in their position. Also, most candidates, much like the business owner themselves, will not have all the skills necessary to do every task in the business. But they might have multiple skills so it is best to know what skills are most important before you start interviewing.

There are also many skills that are required for most every position in the company and including those skills in the list might make it possible to hire a more diversified employee. Other skills can be taught so if your employee turns out to be a great employee you can teach them a couple of new skills to help qualify them for a better position in the future as long as they possess some of the skills from the beginning.

Teaching a new employee required skills can be a time consuming and expensive process so it makes sense to hire people who already possess the needed skills and possibly experience. Every hour spent teaching a new employee skills is a non-productive hour for the employee and time the trainer could have used doing something more productive or important.

What Personal Traits are Important for this Employee?

Many people disregard personality and appearance when it comes to the hiring process. Since it is unlikely that your employee will be working all by his or herself, the need for all your employees to get along with each other as they work is often understated. But when people do not get along with each other, personal productivity goes down and a lot of bickering and in-fighting wastes time.

Also think about how the personality of the employee is going to effect customer service. If the person is involved in direct customer contact you are going to need someone with an out-going and pleasant personality. You want smiling and friendly people in those positions and not angry or nasty people. We want employees who will make customers happy and feel appreciated and we need the personalities to help achieve that.

You also want people who at least appear excited and motivated. You want people who are self-starter and who will work on their own with little supervision and be trusted to get the job done. If someone appears aloof and disinterested at the interview when they are trying to get the job, imagine how they will be once they get it!

As far as appearance is concerned. While there are rules and regulations and a few laws on the books to help companies from discriminating against people you do need to take appearance into consideration in some positions. We are NOT talking about race or sex or anything like that. But if an employee is going to be a visible part of your business he or she should represent your business well.

For example, if you own a physical fitness center and are looking for a personal trainer, you would probably not want to hire a personal trainer who weighs 400 pounds. This is not discriminating against weight or size but having a 400 pound person teaching someone else to lose weight would not likely be inspiring. Your employees should put forth an image that is appropriate for your business. It should inspire customers and give them credibility in the eyes of the customer.

How Many Hours a Week Do You Need Them?

Employees cost money and they need to fulfill a certain function. Part of that function involves the number of hours you are going to need them. Before you interview or hire someone, make sure that you have the money to pay them for the foreseeable future. You do not want to hire someone and spend the time training them only to find out you cannot afford them. That would be bad for both your employee and your business.

What Time of Day Will Your Need Them?

Also think about what portion of the day you are going to need them. Will it be morning, afternoons, evenings or overnights? Different people have different desires when it comes to the times they work and they should understand how well this job will fit into their lives before they accept. Plus, if not mentioned this questions is sure to come up by the employee and you had better know the answer or you will come off looking foolish.

What is Your Target Range for Salary?

Every employee will be paid a salary and at some point in the interview process you are going to have to talk about money. So it is a good idea not to pluck a salary out of thin air or just pay what the going rate is going to be for a few reasons.

You should understand your ability to pay when arriving at a salary. Your business at this point is not likely to have the cash flow to pay someone whatever you or they want to pay them. You need to understand your cash flow and resources to determine what salary to offer the prospective employee.

But you also do not want to offer a lower salary than what everyone else is offering either. You will get what you pay for when it comes to salary. If you offer minimum wage, you will get less qualified people because more qualified and experienced people will demand more money and go where it is available.

Even if you do manage to land a qualified employee at a low salary because they are desperate to get a job, you will run the risk of them leaving as soon as a better paying job comes along. In order to create a satisfied and stable labor force you need to compensate them fairly and equitably.

What is Your Benefit Package?

If you are hiring just a part time employee or two this might not be a factor. But if you are hiring a full-time employee, they are going to expect and demand a certain benefit package. Usual benefits involve sick and vacation time, health insurance, 401K plan and a wide range of other benefits.

So you will need to talk to your lawyer and accountant and set up a benefit package so you can land the best candidates.

In some cases, benefits are just as important, sometimes even more important, than the salary being offered. For this reason put some thought and effort into your benefit package. Though some things like health insurance can be costly, vacation and sick time cost you little other than productivity and could increase the overall value of the position.

Other benefits like allowing your employees to work a flexible schedule often have a huge appeal to people with children or other responsibilities in their lives. It is not so much the value to the business that is important. It is the value the employee places on a specific benefit that really counts.

Demographics and Other Touchy Subjects

OK, here is where we need to be very careful when it comes to hiring employees. You cannot hire people based solely on their race, religion or color. Though there may be times when one person is a better fit than another for certain reasons, those reasons cannot be solely based on any of those mentioned factors and possibly others as well.

Just because you pay their salary does not give the business owner the right or ability to treat them any way they feel like it.

There are labor laws in every state and country and the business owner must act within the confines of those laws. You should know these laws and restrictions before hiring employees to make sure that you do not engage in any kind of discriminatory labor practices.

Responsibilities When You Hire Employees

Up until now your business has been your baby and its success or failure effected just you and your family. You took the profits and felt the losses but your decisions impacted you and your loved ones and very few others.

All that changes when you hire employees. Once there are other people on board you become responsible for them and their financial lives as well. Many of these employees are going to depend on you for their needs. The salary you pay them will provide them with food, shelter, clothes and other things. So your business decisions now effect more people than just yourself and your family. It is a serious responsibility.

Many business owners treat their employees well and their reward is a loyal and stable workforce that works hard for the business.

But there are other business owners who treat their employees poorly and hire and fire them at will and with little regard or consideration given to how their termination has effected the employee's lives.

This is not to say that if your business cannot sustain an employee's costs for any reason that the employee cannot be terminated. But termination should be the last resort and the business owner should understand the seriousness of it before action is taken.

I have worked for people who treated their employees like property and had no problem whatsoever firing people just because they were in the mood to fire someone. I have seen people fired for no reason, certainly not for fiscal or performance based reasons. I even worked for one jerk who fired people every month whether they deserved it or not just to keep everyone else on their toes. Not only was this despicable, it soon cost him his business. And nobody cried for him when it happened. In fact, I'm sure there was a party thrown somewhere to celebrate the demise of the business.

With that being said, here are a few of the responsibilities you are going to have once you hire employees:

You Have to Treat Everyone Fairly

Though this should be a no-brainer, you must treat employees fairly.

You must stay within the laws and guidelines in your area to avoid lawsuits, fines and other legal action. Plus, treat different employees in different ways leads to discontent in the workplace.

That means giving everyone the same treatment and not playing favorites. For example you cannot let one person routinely come in late but dock the pay of another for doing the same thing. Rules need to apply equally and fairly to everyone for the good of the business.

You Have to Obey and Follow Labor Laws

Labor laws are there for a reason and that is to protect the employee and the business from unfair practices. Laws and regulations give the business an established framework that they have to operate within. This allows the business to understand what they can or cannot do when it comes to employee treatment.

Employees benefit because a business cannot do whatever they want with employees just because they pay them a salary. We know that you are not one of the owners that would abuse your employees or take advantage of them but these rules protect them against those who might.

You Have to Pay Taxes and Provide Certain Benefits

We have already talked about benefits but there will also be taxes and record keeping involved in having employees. You will have to work with your accountant to make sure taxes are paid, proper records are kept and that the employees are provided with pay and tax statements as required by law.

You will also have to pay Social Security Taxes (if you operate in the USA) in addition to the other taxes that you pay in your business. It is important that you understand this additional expense as well when it comes to establishing what you can pay the employee versus what the business can afford.

You Need to Create a Stable Workplace

Your business is not just you anymore so you are going to have to do your best to create a workplace environment that is stable and productive. People must feel safe and secure while they are at work so they can be productive and function well in their positions.

We already discussed a bit about being responsible when it comes to hiring and firing and this is one of the most important parts of creating a stable workplace. Contrary to popular opinions, employees do not work best when they fear for their jobs. Though this might be a temporary motivator, eventually employees who are constantly afraid of being terminated will leave to work where there is more stability.

Employees should feel safe and secure both personally and career wise within the company. There should be opportunities for advancement as well as for earning more money when performance dictates. Everyone likes to feel that they can move up and improve themselves at their jobs. If that feeling does not exist people will often not care about doing their best or will leave for a job somewhere else where this is opportunity for advancement.

Always keep in mind that your employees depend on you just like you depend on them. This relationship works best when both the business and the employees are happy with each other. This can only take place when the work environment is created based on mutual respect. It is something that requires constant work and effort both to create and maintain.

You Need to Create Employee Processes and Policies

The more employees you have the more you will find a need to develop employee policies and processes. This is important because you must treat all employee of a certain type the same way and having rules and processes allow you to make everything clear to the employees.

Having an employee handbook that outlines how people are to go about their jobs makes things easier on everyone. Employees have a written document outlining such things as how to report in sick, how to take vacation, vacation black-out period and other items pertaining to the business. Having certain things in writing provides clear guidance on what is and is not acceptable.

Having stated policies and rules often is a requirement under the law when it comes to take disciplinary action or enforcing rules and even for terminating employees. If it is in writing the employee cannot say they were not aware that what they were doing was wrong. If everything is in writing, they cannot use that excuse or defense.

You will find that most employees you hire will be good employees and will not cause you or your business any problems as long as you treat them right. But there will always be one or two who feel they are entitled to more than everyone else and who will take advantage of you at every opportunity. Usually these employees have done this in the past and are well aware of every legal rule or loophole so it is a good idea to make everything as clear as possible to avoid these types of problems.

Employees are part of most businesses and how we go about hiring them and utilizing their skills and talents will be critical to the growth of our business.

But we always need to remember that our employees are also people with the same needs and desires that we have. As long as we treat our employees properly and provide what they need through our business, we will create a stable and loyal labor force.

We also want to keep employees happy because a large or frequent turnover of employees means more time spent interviewing and training new employees which costs the business time and money. Plus, new employees will take time to learn their jobs and become as productive as experienced employees.

Last, but certainly not least, good employees are sometimes difficult to find and once you have one you want to keep them. But if you treat them right, compensate them fairly and give them the ability to improve themselves and their career, you should have no problem keeping your employees for a long, long time.

Remember, employees leave when they find something better for themselves. As long as you represent the best, there is no reason for them to leave. So it just makes sense to become known as a great place to work and a great place to build a career.

Beware of Scams

Unfortunately, any publication on starting your own business would not be complete without at least discussing those people who are ready and willing to take advantage of people and make a quick buck at their expense. Since the majority of people looking to start their own business are doing so because they need or want more money in their lives, these are prime candidates for scammers and con artists.

Think about it for a minute, the majority of people looking to start their own business do so because they have dreams of freedom, riches and independence. These dreams often cloud their judgment and lead to them believing things and claims they otherwise would have clearly questioned. Even though you might not be desperate, people who need more money are the very same people who often try any program or scam out there in the hopes that this is the answer they have been looking and waiting for.

In many cases those same people who need money more than anyone else are the same people who can least afford to lose money. It is to protect those people that we are going to warn you about a few scams and try to get you to look at things more carefully and in a different way.

Here are a few things to consider as you start building your business or when you are considering which business to build:

Claims are Often Bogus

I do not pay much attention to the claims made in business opportunity ads or websites. If you look closely you will see a disclaimer that basically says these claims are not common and you should not expect to earn anywhere near that amount of money and could earn nothing. The fact is, only one person has to earn that amount foe the claim to be valid.

Fortunately these types of claims are being strictly regulated and a lot of them have disappeared lately. But some are still out there and do not get fooled by them. If the basic idea appears to have merit that is one thing. But to make a decision based on claims you see on a website or in an advertisement is never a good idea.

Remember that these claims are designed to "suck in" those people who have a desperate need for money and who are so desperate that they throw reason and common sense out the window and deal with just hope instead.

Get Rich Quick Programs & Opportunities

While it is possible to take a great idea or to think of something no one else has thought before and become an overnight millionaire, it rarely works out that way. Even the millionaires who appeared to get rich overnight usually had put in a lot of time and effort before they achieved their "instant success".

People are rewarded for their ideas or actions or a combination of both. If you have a great idea, you can make money off it. If you make the right moves and do the right things, you can make a lot of money as well. But, to the best of my knowledge, no one has ever made a ton of money without doing any work or having any original thoughts.

You will see all these so-called "business opportunities" which claim to offer instant riches for little or no work. Plus, you can get all of this new and easy income by just paying a one-time $49 fee to the business owner. This kind of "offer" should raise a few red flags in the mind of anyone reading it.

First of all, if something was honestly going to make you millions why is someone selling it for just $49? If I had something that valuable I would either franchise it out for a percentage of the revenue or make it a lot more expensive.

Secondly, if something was really that good and that easy, why would I share it in the first place? I would share it to family and friends and we would all make a boatload of money. That would make sense to me not selling it to anyone who wants it for just $49.

The "I want to help others" Ploy

If you read this and honestly believe it then I guess you deserve everything that happens to you. This is where the owner of the offer tells you they are sharing this wonderful and amazing secret because they are so lucky and so rich that they want to give back to others and help them succeed. What pure BS! If I already have this money why don't I just give it away to people instead of charging them for it?

And that leads us to the next piece of BS where they tell you they charge for it to make sure that only serious people get in on this secret. Supposedly this would keep under motivated people from making money as well. Why that is so important I'm not sure other than to create a BS answer to a very legitimate question.

FREE vs. Fee-Based

Some programs advertise themselves as being free while others are fee-based. I have conflicting views on which is better.

Common sense tells me that if something has a monthly fee attached to it then the content must have value or people would just cancel after the first month and little money would be made. If you have to pay one up-front fee then it makes no difference if the program is crap because they already have all of your money.

Now if that makes sense to you like it once did to me, here is something that might make you revisit your opinion: Studies have shown that there are a significant number of people who will forget the recurring monthly charges and who never check their checking statements to see the charges. So they keep paying for the program for month even though they think it is crap and they never even use it! So even if something is fee-based is not a guarantee that it is a quality product or program.

Sharing Personal Information

Some so-called "legitimate" programs are nothing more than a scam disguised as a business opportunity to get you to give them personal information such as a Social Security Number, phone number, bank account information or other personal data. This data is then used to hack into your personal accounts and steal your money.

Beware of any program that requires you to furnish significant personal information in order to join the program. Unless they are paying you commissions there should be no reason for you to give bank account information. See more on this below.

Creating a Special E-mail Account

Once you respond to a get rich quick or business advertisement and furnish your e-mail address, your name will be immediately sold to a hoard of other people hawking the same type of products. To avoid clogging up your personal or private e-mail address, create a special e-mail account either on your own server or better yet, on one of the free e-mail services such as Hotmail or Gmail.

Then you can keep all the garbage e-mails on that account while keeping your personal account clear of the crap. Once you are sure something is legit and you really want to, you can always submit a change of e-mail request and change the account over to your personal e-mail. Then you can take the account that gets the 200 garbage messages every day and delete it.

Creating a Special On-Line Bank Account

If your business is an online business, or if your business has an online component to it, you are likely going to be using one of the online payment systems like PayPal. When you want to withdraw funds from these payment systems you usually transfer funds into your bank account. The problem with this is that the payment system, and possibly hackers, will have your bank account information.

What I recommend is that you open an account at your local bank just for your online deposits. Empty your online accounts into this account and then transfer the money out to your regular account. Empty all accounts often so there is never a lot of money in either account. This way your personal account information will be a bit safer and the amount you stand to lose will always be minimal.

Regardless of what accounts you list in which websites, always change your passwords several times a year and make them difficult to remember or figure out. Forget using birthdays or anniversaries or your children's names. Oh, yeah, don't use the word "password" either! It' still one of the most common passwords people use!

One Last Thing to Think About....

Here is something you might ask yourself whenever you see something that appears so easy and so quick that you wonder if it is legitimate.

Today there are so many poor people and people living under the poverty line that live off various social programs and government funds. The government spends billions of dollars every year on making sure these people have a roof over their head and food in their stomachs.

Don't you think it would be a far better idea to just pay each $49 to join one of those programs and become instant millionaires? After all, the program says no experience, no special skills and no work required! So why not let the government enroll everyone and instead of paying subsidies every month instead they could be collecting the taxes all of these new millionaires no owe on their fortunes.

It seems like such a simple solution to a very common and expensive problem. The only problem would be if somehow these programs and businesses were not really what they claim to be.

Ahh, that could be it......

Most Common Reasons Business Fail

I never like to end the content of a book on something negative but the information in this chapter can help you create a stronger business with fewer problems. So in essence, even though this chapter deals with mistakes, learning from those mistakes and avoiding them in your business is actually a huge positive for you.

So with that in mind here are some very common and popular reasons why businesses fail or are not growing at their full potential:

Not Enough Funding

Many a new business has failed and gone out of business because there were not sufficient funds to get it started and sustain it though the initial marketing and building process.

You not only need enough money to start the business you also need enough to pay both the business and owner's expenses through the period during which the business may not supply sufficient revenue.

Other times resources are stretched too thin and important expenses such as marketing and promotion are reduced or eliminated. This is counter-productive as it increases the time the business will require to become known and start generating profits.

Not Enough Commitment

Starting a new business is usually accompanied by excitement and dreams of wealth and prosperity. But the fact is there is a period of hard work and a lot of effort to get from a new business to a successful one. This does not happen overnight and you need to sustain the effort through the initial stages until you start to see positive results.

Many times once the novelty has worn off the owner starts working less and has less enthusiasm. The hard work becomes tedious and then the owner looks for any excuse not to do the things that are required to build a new business.

That is why it is so important to have your business centered around something you enjoy and are good at. This way working seems less like work and it is easier to keep up the work and retain the enthusiasm. If you are doing something just for the money then when the money doesn't come right away you get disenchanted and quit.

Not Detailed Oriented Enough

When you start a new business everything is brand new. Virtually nothing has become a habit as yet and there are so many little things that have to get done in order for the business to run smoothly. If any of these things are misplaced or forgotten it can cause a lot of problems for the business moving forward.

Plus, there will be times when things have to be done in a specific order so that the next item on the list can be acted upon as well. For example, if you do not submit your advertising in time to meet a deadline then the ad will not run when you want it to. This can be weeks or even months in advance.

All of this requires a detail oriented approach to management. If you are not detail oriented them take steps to organize everything you need to do in a daily or monthly planner so you are always being reminded of what has to be done and in what or and by what date.

Failure to handle all the little details will often cause the big things to fall through the cracks and cause problems for the business. There can be missed deadlines, penalties to pay or interest to be paid when things aren't paid on time. All of these little things can add up to huge problems for you and your business.

Quit too Soon

Sometimes people do all the right things in the right order but just don't keep at it long enough for good results to come around. Establishing a new business takes patience and it takes time. You need to get your business out in front of the customer and give them time to see what you are all about and to finally become comfortable enough to purchase from you.

Give yourself a legitimate time frame and work hard throughout that time to get your business recognized. Volunteer in public events, promote and advertise your business and do whatever it takes to make sure your business becomes known to the public. If you have a great product or offer a great service that people need, they eventually will purchase it from you. But only if you keep up the f=efforts until you become known in your area or on the internet.

Exactly how much time is not accurately known but the rule of thumb should be the more expensive your products are the longer it will take people to feel comfortable enough to buy from you compared to a more well know and established business. People will be far more willing to take a chance on buying a loaf of bread from you than they will be buying a new $20,000 vehicle from a brand new dealer.

Waited too Long

On the flip side, not every product is a slam dunk winner and even the best ideas sometimes fall flat on their face. The key is to know the difference between waiting long enough for a product or service to catch on and waiting too long before pulling the plug on it. Continuing to throw more money and more effort on a dead idea or product is just not smart.

If you are working for months to try and get something established and are starting to see a trickle or increase of sales that could tell you that there is a demand or market out there for what you are selling. But if you have worked for 6 months to a year and have yet to close a single sale or have not received any positive activity from your efforts, it might be time to rethink your idea and pull the plug.

Personal belief in a product or service is not a reason to keep on trying and pouring money down the drain. Sometimes we become so personally attached or emotionally invested that we fail to see that no one else wants what we think is so great. When you do realize that you need to chalk it up to experience and pull the plug and move on. The result will be saving resources to be better used on the next idea or situation and not continue to waste resources where they will do little good.

Not Enough Advertising

You cannot expect people to come to your business if they do not know that you even exist. You have to get your business out there in front of the public and advertising and marketing is how you accomplish that.

You cannot expect people to search high and low for you. You have to be in their face and tell them why they should buy from you instead of where they are currently buying. People need reasons to change something that is currently working for them. Advertising does just that be showing them what you have to offer and why you are the better choice.

People have to be shown why they should buy from you. You cannot expect them to connect the dots, you have to connect them for him. Well-designed advertising and a well-constructed marketing campaign will do that for you. It will showcase your business and what makes it special.

Without advertising you will be relying on people just randomly finding you or by the slow growth or word of mouth advertising. This will take a long time and result in a long time before your business every shows a profit if it ever does. Cutting advertising is one of the first things some business owners do when money gets tight and that is just counter-productive.

Poor Brand Reputation

A good business is more than just a great product or line of products. A great business is a BRAND. Your brand is what makes your business special or desirable in the mind of the customer. If your brand reputation is poor then your business is going to suffer and it will be harder to bring customers through your doors.

Many things make up a brand and businesses that do not create a strong and positive brand image usually do not stay in business for very long. The products and services and the customer experience are all part of your brand. You MUST do your very best with every aspect of the business to create a very strong and positive brand image.

A powerful brand will also improve word of mouth advertising and help bring more people through your front doors. But a weak or negative brand image will do exactly the opposite and drive people away from your business and to your competition.

Poor Brand Recognition

As we said, businesses are all about brands and not just products. If the business owner concentrates on just the products they sell and not on brand recognition, the business will suffer and might even ultimately fail.

Most of the time there will be options to the customer for the products and services you sell. What makes you different is your brand. If people don't understand why your brand is better because you haven't made the effort to tell them, then your business is likely to suffer. Most people will not buy something they need from someone they do not perceive has a good brand. You might get a sale or two based on convenience but no one is going to go out of their way when they do not see the benefit in doing so.

Lack of Focus

Starting and building a business requires a lot of focus.

By that we mean being able to get things done in the right way and watching out to make sure everything that is supposed to happen does happen. Some business owners allow themselves to lose focus when they start on the next new or exciting project.

It is very easy to start an internet business, develop a website and then just forget about it when you get the next product idea. We have all done it and it has hurt many a business. You need to stay engaged and focused on the details of your business in order for it to succeed. You need to constantly try to make things better, spend your money wisely and make the sacrifices almost every small business owner makes in the beginning.

Building a business is a process. Early on almost nothing runs on autopilot and it takes a while for that to occur. Once it does things get easier but in the beginning, the owner must remain totally focused on their business or bad things will start to happen.

Too Much Diversification

When you start your business, you have a certain business plan. Some business owners make the mistake of creating way too a diverse business plan in order to capture as wide a market share as possible. Usually this is a mistake.

Your business is going to be built around a product or group of products in a single market. You might sell furniture or books or kitchen devices or you might provide cleaning services or some other service. That is where your efforts should be directed. You should develop and build your brand not over expand.

Suppose you sell self-help books and you are doing OK but not great. So you decide to also sell sweaters as well. So now you have one website or store that sells books and now sweaters. Those two products have nothing to do with one another and will confuse your customers and weaken your brand.

Sometimes even over expanding a complimentary line of products can be dangerous as well. Expanding anything too quickly can cost a LOT of money and take a lot of time. It can also cause a lot of problems as well. People who try to expand their business too fast or in the wrong ways often run out of capital and do not have the manpower or resources to adequately support the expanded business.

It is much better to concentrate on building your core business and then expand a little bit at a time so the process is manageable and controlled. The last thing a business needs to do expend so rapidly that service suffers and what was once special or unique about the business no longer exists.

Once your business has lot what made it unique your customers may no longer have the need to buy from you. Other businesses might suddenly become more attractive as your brand weakens. Expansion is good for your business when it can be done properly and remain controlled. But even in that situation, always try to keep your business true to what your customers like about it. Otherwise you and your expanded business could very well find itself in need of rapid contraction back to where it all began. And sometimes even that isn't possible.

Lack of Expertise

For a business to be successful, people who run it need to have the expertise to not only run the business but create it and design it properly. There are many "hats" the new business owner has to wear and they might not have all the skills and activities that are needed to properly create and run the business. But that doesn't mean that everyone cannot start their own business. It just means that some of us will need a bit of help.

It is rare for one person to be exceptional in every part of the business. Smart business owners understand their strengths and also their weaknesses. But the smart business owner does something that some owners refuse to do.

They ask for help or they look for help.

Granted there will be times when money is tight but there are ways to get help at little or no cost if you just try hard enough to find it. You can go to local businesses and ask questions or join a business group. You might take a class or course to turn a weakness into a strength. It makes no difference whether you do everything yourself or have other people help you handle a few of the things.

It is not a sign of weakness to ask for help. In fact, many consider asking for help to be a strength because it means the person is placing results above their pride when it comes to their business. So it can be said that a strong man asks for help while the weaker man hangs on to his pride above all else.

If you need help, go out and find it. If you have a weakness, find help or learn and turn that weakness into a strength. But regardless of the path you choose, do not stay where you are and think you can do everything.

Because you can't

Summary

Business fail each and every day. But a lot of business succeed as well and it is up to you what happens to you and your business.

But you should also be aware that there are also going to be things that occur that were totally unexpected and seemingly out of your control. It is easy to beat yourself up over these things.

But if there was one piece of advice that I could give you it would be to worry and concern yourself about the things that you have control over. Obsess over what you can change and make better and let the other stuff happen. Because if you don't, you are going to wind up with some serious health issues and you will not enjoy life or your business.

Every business has things that are out of the control of the owner. You can have the best products and killer advertising and marketing and the best stores and you can sell at the lowest prices. But there still will come a point where you have to put all of that out there and hope that it is enough to make the customers come to you.

There is no store layout or website layout that makes people buy. There is no legal thing you can do to force people to buy from you as compared to buying somewhere else. All you can do is your best with what you have control over.

If, at the end of the day, you can say that you did your best, then be happy with that.

If you have done your absolute best and it wasn't good enough, you can live with that. But what you cannot live with is taking the easy way, slacking off and then blaming your business failures on someone else. Always do your best so that when you look back after something went wrong you can say you did your best.

You can live with that.

Learning from your Mistakes

I've got some bad and good news for you when it comes to starting your own business. The bad news is that no matter how hard you try and no matter how good your intentions are, you are going to make mistakes. The good news is that no matter how hard you try and no matter how good your intentions are, you are going to make mistakes!

It's not so much if you are going to make a mistake it is just a matter of when those mistakes are going to happen. The most important thing is not so much the mistakes you are going to make but what happens after you make the mistake that matters most.

People who make mistakes and learn from those mistakes are the same people who create hugely successful companies because they learn valuable knowledge from what they did wrong.

They do something that doesn't work out the way they thought and they break it down to see what might have been done differently or better. Then the next time they do things differently and get better results.

It is the people who fail to learn from their mistakes who have the biggest problem. If you do the same thing over and over and get the same results, things are never going to change. Unless you change what you are doing, you are going to get the same result. To think things will be any different is lunacy!

Here is how you can learn from your mistakes and get the best results in the shortest period of time. All you need to do is always follow the following 3 step process:

Act, Test, Revise & Repeat

This is one of the easiest to explain scientific principles as far as learning is concerned. It is one of the most common methods of learning and every one of us has used it from the time we were born. The system consists of three parts, act, test, and revise. Everything we learn in life uses this process. And now we are going to use this same process and apply it to starting and running our own business.

Act

We are going to take action and do something for our business. This might be creating a product, running an ad, making a deal or anything that is going to help out business grow. We all know if we want something to change or happen we need to take action. So step one is taking the action.

Test

After taking the action, we need to test what we have done to see if it had the desired result. If it did, then we are good to go and our actions have been proven satisfactory and we can move on. But if they didn't get the results we expected or needed then we are going to have to figure out why that happened.

So we take our action and figure out how to see if it had the desired result. If we created an advertisement, how well did it perform? Did it get the anticipated number of new sales? Did it get more or less than we hoped? This will determine what we do next.

Revise & Repeat

If something didn't go well or as planned then we have to look at what we did and change something. It might be a little change or a massive one. It really doesn't matter. But we determine what went wrong, what the most likely cause was, and we change something to get a better result.

This is caused revising our actions. This means we are going to try again but we are going to do something different this time so that we get better or different results. Then after deciding what we have to do, we go back to step one and enact those changes. And then we go through the 3 steps again.

Sometimes we need to go through this several times before we get things right. It really doesn't matter how many times as long as we make progress. But we should only change one thing at a time so we know whether something works better or not. If we change two things and one works better and the other works worse, we might see no change because they cancelled each other out. So just change one thing at a time and monitor the results.

Here is a common example that every one of us can relate to. When every one of us learned to walk as infants, we used this process. Here is how it went:

Act: We took a step

Test: We fell on our face. That didn't work so well.

Revise: So we decided to take a different step.

Repeat

Act: We take a different step.

Test: And still fell on our face but it took a bit longer.

Revise: We made one final change to our step and balance.

Repeat

Act: We take another step.

Test: We don't fall!

Revise: No revisions necessary. We just practice now!

You can apply this to almost anything you have done in life. Trying to hit a ball or catch a ball. Learning how to play a musical instrument. We all make mistakes the first few times we try something. But we continually change what we are doing and monitoring our results. We gradually get better and efforts become successful and then those efforts become habits and we do those same things without thinking. This is how people learn and this is how people learn how to grow their businesses as well.

The most important thing to understand is that it is all right to make mistakes as long as you learn from them. It is one thing to make a mistake and learn from it and another thing to keep making the same mistakes over and over and over again. You have control over what you do and how you learn.

Which means you have a choice to make. Are you going to make mistakes and learn from them or are you going to keep making those same mistakes all through your life.

We have all seen people continue to make the same mistakes because they refuse to admit they made a mistake. Call it pride or call it delusion but it is very sad. Because people who never admit their mistakes and take responsibility for them never learn and never get better.

So admit your mistakes, admit that you are going to make more mistakes in the future and then learn as much as you can when those mistakes happen. Because you cannot eliminate mistakes but you can always take advantage of them.

Quick Start Guide

Now that you have the basics
and a lot of information to get you
started, here are a few things to
help you start creating the business
you need right now!

Starting Your $50 Business

Many people have started their profitable businesses on a shoestring with little or no money down. There are many ways to do this and the only limitations are your own imagination and the law! After all, you want to build your business the right way and that means always doing what's right and staying within the law.

With a small cash outlay like $50 you are limited to two main business models. Those are working out of your home and operating an online business. After all you will not have money for rent or to build a building for your business so we need to work with what we have available.

If you are going to start with just $50 then you are probably going to have to sell some kind of service, someone else's product such as an affiliate marketing product or sell your own product that is inexpensive to produce.

A perfect product might be an information book or other book that could be produced digitally and sent via e-mail at no cost. Many a successful business has been built in this manner.

As we have already stated, you can easily start an online business for less than $50. The first thing you will need to do is purchase a domain name. You can get a domain in the .com extension for about $10-$12 now at Godaddy.com. Pick a good name that people will remember when it comes to getting back to your website.

In the beginning, if you have several products in the same niche or industry then consider a generic domain name such as Elitekitchenrecipes.com which would cover books on all kinds of recipes. As your business grows and more money is being made you could then go to a domain name for every book or product using that books title as the domain name. But for now, unless you can get a better and more specific name, go generic so you can sell multiple products on one site.

The second step is to find a hosting account which you can do by searching for hosting companies. Hostgator is one and they have hosting for about $5 per month or in that ballpark. Register for a hosting plan and then go into where you purchased your domain name and change the name servers to point your domain to your hosting company.

Once you have completed those steps you have spent about $20 and you are officially in business! Anything you build on your domain will not be seen by anyone coming to that domain.

Now you need to create your website. You can either use WordPress which comes with almost any hosting plan or you can use some of the pre-built websites that come with many hosting plans. Of course, if you know anything about web design, you can always build your own website.

If you are selling affiliate products then all the order taking and fulfillment will be done by the affiliate company. All you do is cash your commission checks. But if you are selling your own products, and are not selling them through any kind of service, you will have to sign up for PayPal (free!) or use a product fulfillment system to deliver your digital product to your customers.

Of course, if you are selling physical products you will have to mail the products to the customer yourself. If that is your business model then you will have to spend a few dollars on mailing boxes or envelopes to ship your products in.

If you have any money left over you can purchase some paid traffic to give your business a little boost but search carefully. Quality traffic can be costly but there are a few bargains out there.

But even if you don't have any money left you can promote your website on blogs and social media for free. The one great thing about the internet is that there are a lot of free ways to promote that just take your time.

As of now you have a legitimate business up on the internet with a website full of content and ready to take orders. All for less than $50! It might take a little while to get your first order or that first order might come within the first hour. It all depends on your domain name, your website and your products. But you can refine all that you have done to make it bigger, better and more relevant.

One mistake a lot of internet businesses make is trying to have everything perfect before releasing your site. Trust me when I say that your website will NEVER be perfect! There will always be something that can be made better or some new technology that will allow you to make better changes and improved functionality.

So get something basic done and get it out on the internet. Let the search engines find it. Then, once you have something on your website, then work on improving it. The great thing about an online business is that changes can be made almost instantaneously. You make the change, upload it and everything is done right away. No waiting for changes to be implemented.

So if something needs improvement, you can change it right away. If you discover a problem you can fix it right away. There is no real reason to wait for perfection that never will come. Put together a site that looks nice so people will like it but don't try to hit a home run the first time you go to bat.

For those of you interest in creating your own website, there are page builder software programs available that allow you to do a "drag n drop" website very quickly. These can get pricy but there are some free and lower cost ones out there as well. Search, learn and pick the one that's right for you.

Brick & Mortar Business Building

If you wish to build a local business catering to local cliental then at first you are probably going to work from home. A home based business is convenient and practical for stay at home moms and other people who wish to try their hand at a business without risking a lot of money.

If you want to start a business out of your home all you really need is a few flyers or letter describing your business and a way of getting those flyers into the hands of people in your area. You can walk the neighborhood yourself and deliver the fliers or you can mail them.

Mailing can get expensive really fast and you would not be able to mail out a lot of fliers for your $50 so I would look into other means of delivery.

You could place fliers under windshield wipers at the mall or place signs on telephone poles if allowed in your area. Depending on what products or services you are offering, you will have to find the right method of advertising to get to the people you want to reach. A new home-based business is all about marketing and advertising and getting your name and business out there to the people who need it.

You can put a sign on the window of your car so people see it as you drive around town. If your home is on a main street or road just placing a sign on your front lawn might be a good idea as well. The more people you can make aware of your business the faster it will become established and grow. It is all in the marketing and promotion.

Remember we talked about volunteering in your community? That is a great way for brand new home-based businesses to get noticed in the community. Spend a little bit of time and effort doing those things you need to do in order to get your business recognized. With just a little bit of money at the start you are going to have to do more of this kind of activity than you will later. Sometimes even going door to door will be what it takes to get your business off the ground and growing.

Even though you have a home-based business do not discount the value of having a website as well. More and more people today search online first before looking in the phone books. Some people only look online so if you do not have an online presence, really consider getting one. One very nice business model is using part of your $50 to create an online presence first and then start advertising on a local level as well. Since many people will remember your name, they might search for you online first to see what kind of business you are talking about. Having an online presence will add credibility to you and your business.

Other Expenses

You may have other expenses not counted in the $50 such as the cost of local licenses and any insurance, if required in your area. Make sure you have what you need to create your business and remain in compliance with all local and federal laws and regulations. We have said it a few times already but ignorance is not an effective defense.

How Should You
Spend Your Money?

One of the most common problems or questions new or fledgling business owners has is how do they spend the limited amount of money they have available to them when they are starting their business. Since sometimes these funds are very limited (the $50 start-up for example) it is important that they are used wisely to help the business in the most efficient ways possible.

While every business is different and every owner will find themselves in a slightly different situation, it is not possible to give you a specific blueprint on where to spend every dollar. But we can give you a way to determine the very best way to spend however much money you do have available.

When starting your business, or at any time during the operation of your business when you have a financial decision to make, divide all your expenses into three groups.

Those three groups should be **required expenses, needed expenses** and **discretionary expenses.** Here is an explanation of each group:

Required Expenses

These are the expenses that your business must have to either stay afloat or to keep within the law. Examples of these types of expenses would be rent, taxes, licensing fees or renewals, salaries or payroll, invoices for inventory or other expenses with a fixed due date.

There is really no other option than to pay these expenses on time or before their due date to remain in compliance or to avoid late fees or collection fees. Also included would be invoices from suppliers which you want to pay on time so that you keep the right relationship with these people. Paying late might cause them to stop sending you goods and services in the future and that will hurt your business.

If you find that you cannot pay these expenses because you do not have the required funds, then contact those that you cannot pay and ask for an extended payment deadline. With the exception of the government, most people will work with you and will understand a temporary cash flow problem. But their understanding will only work if these requests are made very rarely.

Do not plead poverty when you have the funds just to avoid paying them. This will quickly destroy any relationship you have with anyone or any company.

Needed Expenses

These are the expenses that you need to take care of to keep your business running smoothly but ones that you have a bit of "wiggle room" when it comes to when you incur them. Examples of these kinds of expenses might be advertising costs, an improvement to your business, graphics design costs, new product development costs and other costs that are important but might be able to be put off for a while until cash flow improves.

These are the expenses that you need to have and you should not stop incurring those expenses because they are important to your business. But unlike fixed expenses such as rent or tax payments, you have some control on when you incur them. This is an important part of managing your business.

Every business needs advertising and no business owner should stop advertising to save money. After all advertising helps bring in new customers and create new sales. So every dollar you spend on advertising, if it is effective, should result in several dollars of revenue coming back to the business.

In some cases it might actually make sense to spend more money on advertising when things are tight because of the revenue advertising generates.

Sometimes we can schedule these expenses so that they hit our books at the best time of the month. For example if rent and tax payments are due by the 1st of the month then we can purchase our advertising on the 15th of the month. This way all the expenses do not hit all at once. You still have to pay all of your bills but the due dates can be staggered to make it easier.

Discretionary Expenses

These are the expenses that might be nice to have, or might help you in the future but your business doesn't really need them at this point. These are the expenses that are invisible to the customer so you could put them off or eliminate them completely.

Examples of these expenses might be a coffee machine for the office or someone to come in and clean up at the end of the day. That is something you might consider doing yourself when money is tight. Or perhaps you are looking to re-design your store or website but your existing website or store is fine the way it is for right now.

Every business has things they would like to buy or do but can't because the money just isn't there. It is up to the business owner to decide which expenses are absolutely necessary and which are not crucial to the development and well-being of the business.

Though the business owner might not like it or want to hear it, taking a salary might fall under this type of heading because as a business owner you should share in the profits but when there are no profits you should not be taking a salary out of the business. Those funds should go towards the expenses of the business. You would then start taking a salary again when cash flow improves.

Personal Credit Expenses

We are listing credit expenses under their own heading because credit expense are a different kind of expenses with their own flexibility and hidden dangers. Many new business owners finance some part of their new business with their personal credit cards. These cards might be used to purchase goods or materials to start the business or for ease of on-going payments from online vendors. Either way the business owner need to use credit wisely and carefully.

Credit card debt is flexible in that you can have the option to pay all or just part of the bill each month.

So if you run into a month where cash flow is very tight, you can take your personal credit card debt and pay just a portion of it and carry the rest over to the next month. Doing so will not hurt your credit rating unless you have a lot of money outstanding on the account.

While this is an attractive option to have when it comes to managing money, it is a dangerous one as well. Credit card interest is among the highest forms of interest sometimes exceeding 20% and in some cases 30% for some cards. Paying this interest rate on business purchases is like paying 20% more on all your purchases! It just makes no sense to pay this high interest if you can possibly avoid it.

If you are able to pay your full balance at the end of every billing cycle and not pay any interest, credit cards give you another great option when it comes to managing debt. Depending on when you make your purchases you can extend the payment time by up to 4-6 weeks by careful planning, This is sometimes referred to as "floating" and it can help you manage expenses much easier.

Let's say your credit card billing period ends on the 2nd day of the month. Items you purchase on the 1st of the month will be on your next bill which will be due at the end of the month. This gives you a couple of week before you have to pay those charges.

But if you hold off and purchase something on the 3rd of the month, just two days later, those charges will not appear for another month when you get your next bill and then you have another few weeks after that to pay them!

So if you have to make a purchase and you can schedule it to get the most float on your money, that might help you make ends meet and do more for your business. But there are two things you need to remember whenever you use this strategy.

First, you still have to pay for whatever you purchase and credit card debt can easily sneak up on you if you are not very careful. So even though you have the extra time to use the money, eventually all bills need to be paid. So be very careful and never charge more than you are fairly sure you will be able to pay back on time.

Second, this strategy does not work if you carry over any portion, no matter how small, of your bill on any given month. Whenever you carry a balance you are them paying full interest **from the date of purchase** on ALL your charges both your existing balance and any new purchases. So when you have a balance and are paying interest charges you have **zero float** and this can cause you a ton of problems later on.

Summary

Every business owner needs to be somewhat of an accountant and manage not only their personal finances but the finances of the business as well. If you have an accountant they can help you manage your cash flow and advise you but it is the day to day expenses and how those are managed that can make the difference between a successful business and a bankrupt business.

Managing money so that you can do everything your business needs to make it grow is sometimes challenging. We often have the urge to stop advertising or marketing and save those expenses but as we already stated, such actions are not prudent and will just make things worse in the long run.

So they key is using your money wisely and planning your expenses carefully so that you have the best chances of getting the most from your money. Go ever your expenses and note when they are due every month. Then take steps to spread out as many of the expenses as you can over the month so that there is not one time when everything is due all at once. If you take the time to manage you money your money will be able to do more for you and your business.

Investing in Your Business

As your business grows and starts generating profits, you are going to be tempted to take those profits out of the business and use them. While you certainly are entitled to the profits of your hard fought labors, keep in mind that every business needs some money to expand and grow. As the owner of the business, that money usually comes out of your pocket.

I would recommend that you take a certain percentage right off the top for reinvesting in your business. The actual figure or amount would depend on what you can afford and what your current financial situation might be. But even just 10% reinvesting can help a business grow and prepare itself for the future.

Just like we save for the future and set aside money for little things life throws our way, so must a business owner [put a little bit away as well.

Equipment breaks, builds get damaged, people steal stuff and refunds always seem to come at the wrong time. So having some money going back into the business to help the business grow and to prepare it for the future is always a good thing.

I always recommend paying the business first and making a standard deduction every month into a special business account dedicated to expansion and the future. Pay the business first and then take out your profits. This way you never see the money so you actually never get a chance to miss it. What is left over is your profits and that is all you see.

In addition, you should always be setting aside money for maintenance and upgrades. There is always new software upgrades that are needed as well as constant changes to your buildings and websites to keep them state of the art and impressive for the customer. These are all on-going expenses that should be budgeted for as well.

All of this takes a bit of discipline and practice. In the early stages when money is tight this can be very difficult to do on a regular basis. But you need to hold steady and invest back into your business so it will always be able to grow and be current.

For this we need money and it might mean purchasing a new software program instead of going out for dinner and then to a show. This is where the discipline comes in.

Work with your accountant to come up with a savings and re-investment plan that makes sense for you and your business. This way your business will continue to grow and the profits will continue to rise until the profits are so large you won't mind reinvesting at all. But it takes time to get there and it takes discipline.

Beware of FREE Resources!

Regardless of what type of business you are starting or thinking about starting, there will always be some free resources that will become available to you. While some of these resources might be good, you need to be really careful about some of the ones out there. Because there is no such thing as free no matter how you slice it.

The exception might be some of the government sponsored services such as mentoring programs and other similar types of programs. These are good and you should take advantage of them. Most of them are funded through either government funding or through private sponsored funding. If what you are looking for is knowledge and assistance, these programs might be a great place to start.

But some of the other so-called "free" programs are not all that free and those that are might have little to nothing to offer you. When it comes to preserving and enhancing your brand and brand image, you need to be careful about where your brand is seen and with what it is being seen with.

For example, you might wish to save a few dollars and go with a free e-mail account. While there is nothing wrong with that, if there are messages attached to your e-mails that cheapens your brand. Plus, if you use on of the free e-mail services and it is well-known as a free e-mail that can really cheapen your brand in the eyes of the consumer. They might notice the free e-mail and wonder what kind of company uses a free e-mail in their business? When it comes to e-mail, create one on your own hosting account for brand enhancement and other factors.

The same goes for a free hosting account. Someone somewhere is doing something to make money offering those free services. Usually they make their money by embedding ads into your site or e-mails. So right there next to your product sales pitch you might see an ad for a competing products or something selling something wonderful like an erectile dysfunction product. For these reasons if at all possible stay away from free hosting as well.

Free traffic is one of those areas where you might say you have nothing to lose but the time it takes to fill out the form requesting the ad or traffic. Though there might be slight damage done to your brand traffic is only as good as who sees it. If your webpages are shown to people who are likely to use your product, that is great. But if they are shown places where no one goes, that's not so great.

One thing I have always had a problem with was why someone who had high quality and targeted traffic that delivered sales would give that away for free? Most of us would gladly pay for it yet they are giving it away! Why? Maybe because it is not good quality traffic at all. At least that has been my thought.

I would say that if you can get free exposure or traffic where people who use your product are usually going to then go for it. After all, what do you have to lose? Unless the traffic provider is looking for your information you have little to use.

I always use a special e-mail for these so-called "free services." I would set up and e-mail address such as free@yourdomain.com when you sign up so they will not have access to your real e-mail. If they ask for a lot of personal information, just pass on signing up. Otherwise you can use your "free" e-mail address you created.

Free items like page builder and web hosts can add their own content to your webpages and this is not good for brand identity either. If you think that this might be one of the catches you should look at your pages to see if any content has been added. If it has they drop the free service immediately.

Free services can help the new business owner by making certain services and products within their grasp even though finances are tight. But they have some trade-offs that users need to be aware of. Use them if you want but be careful and do not expect much in the way of quality or performance. After all, if something really was that good, people would charge for it and most of us would be happy to pay for it!

Conclusion

Well, here we are. We have given you a lot of information and you might be a little overwhelmed about some or all of it and perhaps even a bit frightened as well. But let me reassure you that you can do this and you can create and operate a successful business. It has been done and it can be done again if you have what it takes.

Perhaps the most difficult thing to do is take that first step. For most of us that is the toughest thing. We are afraid of failure and we are afraid of losing money. Both are legitimate fears and we have gone to great lengths to address both of those fears so they will not stand between you and your dreams.

We have told you how to get started for less than $50 and everyone should be able to risk that much for a life's worth of freedom. Almost everyone can afford to lose the $50 if something goes wrong so you should not be crippled with feat over that.

As far as failure is concerned, those who never have failed have never really tried. Most of success stems from initial failure. Thomas Edison had 100's of failed prototypes of the electric light until he finally found one that worked. Imagine if he had been afraid of e=fear when he started?

I urge everyone reading this book to take that first step. It can be a small step like purchasing a domain name or it can be a large step and start creating your own product to market to others. I don't care what that first step is. The only important part is that you take it.

Though it's sad to say, a large percentage of people who purchased this book will never take that step. In fact, a large percentage of people who purchased this book will never even complete it so it is unlikely they are even reading this page. It isn't because the book is not well written because it is a work of art (☺) but simply because people start something and lose interest right away so they never take action.

You, on the other hand, have already taken the first step by purchasing this book and then actually reading it and learning from it. So right off the bat you have an advantage over a lot of other people because you have already done something. You have taken that all important first step.

So now let's follow that with steps 2, 3, and 4. Let's design, create and start our own business. Anyone can do it and we have already shown you that you are better than most people. So there is no reason not to keep going. There is no reason to allow fear or uncertainty keep you from achieving your dreams. There is no valid reason to give up either.

You can do this if you try. Life will change only when you do something differently. You cannot expect to continue doing the same things and expect a different outcome. Life just doesn't work that way. Expecting something to change all by itself is simply insanity.

There have been too many people with dreams that took those dreams and built successful businesses to believe that this cannot happen to you. It can happen if you are willing to pursue your dreams and do what is necessary to turn those dreams into reality. I've said this over and over. You can do this. You can succeed. So just try. Just commit yourself to your dreams.

And then watch your future change.

Just stand back and watch!

Resource Page

For information on Business and Customer Service,

Please go to:

The Customer Service Training Institute

http://www.infowhse.com

For How-to and Self-Improvement information,

Please go to:

26 Ways.com

http://www.26ways.com